ANTIQUE to HEIRLOOM
Jelly Roll Quilts

ANTIQUE to HEIRLOOM
Jelly Roll Quilts

12 MODERN QUILT PATTERNS FROM VINTAGE PATCHWORK QUILT DESIGNS

PAM & NICKY LINTOTT

David and Charles

CONTENTS

Introduction

Over the past thirty years since opening The Quilt Room in Dorking we have accumulated a collection of antique quilts from both sides of the Atlantic and we love everything about them. There is nothing more inspiring than seeing the quilts of bygone days, and having them on display in the shop has been a treat for staff and customers alike. A number of them are showing some wear and tear and their colours are a little faded but it does nothing to diminish their beauty – in fact it only enhances their appeal.

We have often considered using some of the patterns from these antique quilts to make modern-day versions and gradually the idea took hold. The fact that most of the quilts have a scrappy look to them made the use of a jelly roll perfect. But could we make these patterns from jelly rolls? You bet we could! We also have friends with gorgeous antique quilts and made the most of this when choosing patterns to make for this book.

Our antique quilts are all bed size and as we only wanted to use 'just one jelly roll' in each quilt we wondered how we would get around this. As it turned out it was a win-win situation as the array of different colours in each quilt comes from the jelly roll and the addition of extra background fabric allowed us to create bed size quilts, which we felt was important for our 'today's heirloom' quilts.

The antique quilts were our inspiration and our modern-day quilts are as near as possible to the antique version, although we have allowed ourselves some artistic licence. Most of our antique quilts didn't have labels so we cannot give the makers the credit due to them. We can only thank all those anonymous quilters of the past for the inspiration they have given us. We hope you will enjoy browsing through our selection of antique quilts and, more importantly, we hope you enjoy creating your very own heirloom quilts.

Getting Started

WHAT IS A JELLY ROLL?

A jelly roll is a roll of forty fabrics cut in 2½in wide strips across the width of the fabric. Moda introduced jelly rolls to showcase new fabric ranges. How inspirational to have one 2½in wide strip of each new fabric wrapped up so deliciously! If you want to make any of the jelly roll quilts in this book and don't have a jelly roll to use, then cut a 2½in wide strip from forty fabrics in your stash and you can follow all the instructions in just the same way. Our patterns are based on a jelly roll strip being 42in long.

IMPERIAL OR METRIC?

Jelly rolls from Moda are cut 2½in wide and at The Quilt Room we have continued to cut our strip bundles 2½in wide. When quilt making, it is impossible to mix metric and imperial measurements. It would be absurd to have a 2½in strip and tell you to cut it 6cm to make a square! It wouldn't be square and nothing would fit. This caused a dilemma when writing instructions for the quilts and a decision had to be made. All our instructions therefore are written in inches. To convert inches to centimetres, multiply the inch measurement by 2.54. For your convenience, any extra fabric you will need, given in the Requirements panel at the start of the quilt instructions, is given in both metric and imperial.

SEAM ALLOWANCE

We cannot stress enough the importance of maintaining an accurate *scant* ¼in seam allowance throughout. Please take the time to check your seams with the test in General Techniques.

QUILT SIZE

In this book we show what can be achieved with just *one* jelly roll. We have added background fabric and borders but the basis of each quilt is just one jelly roll. The size of our quilts is therefore restricted to this fact but there is nothing to stop you using more fabric and increasing the size of your quilt. The Vital Statistics in each chapter gives you all the information you need to enable you to do some simple calculations to make a larger quilt.

Scattered throughout the book there are features called Heirloom Quilt Ideas, giving suggestions on how you might alter the quilt designs. You would, however, need to amend the fabric requirements if changing the quilt layout.

DIAGRAMS

Diagrams have been provided to assist you in making the quilts and these are normally beneath or beside the relevant stepped instruction. The direction in which fabric should be pressed is indicated by arrows on the diagrams. The reverse side of the fabric is shown in a lighter colour than the right side. Read all the instructions through before starting work on a quilt.

WASHING NOTES

It is important that pre-cut fabric is *not* washed before use. Save the washing until your quilt is complete and then make use of a colour catcher in the wash or possibly dry clean.

SPECIALIST TOOLS USED

For cutting half-square triangles from strips we use the Multi-Size 45/90 and the Multi-Size 45/60 from Creative Grids, which have markings that refer to the *finished* size. If you are using a different ruler when cutting half-square and quarter-square triangles please make sure you are using the correct markings before cutting.

SWEET SIXTEEN

Antique Inspiration

The 1930s was a time of great economic upheaval, with the 1929 stock market crash in America heralding a decade of hard times called the Great Depression. This American quilt dates back to those times but is anything but depressing, with its bright colours and simple design. Quilters who couldn't afford to buy new fabrics sought inspiration from magazines and created many inventive designs from fabric scraps, recycled clothing and feedsack materials. Block designs with small pieces, such as Bow Tie, Irish Chain and Drunkard's Path became popular as they allowed quilters to ensure that even the smallest scraps of fabric were not wasted. Colour choices became lighter and brighter than the previously more sombre Colonial style.

This charming quilt has sixteen-patch blocks made up of sixteen small squares of different fabrics, alternating with light plain squares, and would have been a popular design to create from scrap fabrics. The quilt was bought as a quilt top while we were on a trip to the Quilt Market in Houston, USA. We backed it with a plain calico and then longarm quilted it in a medium-sized feather design. The quilt measures 75in x 86in (191cm x 219cm).

Today's Heirloom

For our modern-day quilt it would have been very easy to use a bright and cheerful reproduction 1930s range of fabrics combined with white. The result would have looked stunning and authentic and this is an option you might consider. However, we decided instead to make our heirloom quilt in warm, creamy fabrics and chose a jelly roll from Fig Tree & Co called Buttercup. This range has a lovely mix of blue, peach, pink, mint green and light brown, and when alternated with a creamy tone-on-tone fabric it created a quilt that made you feel warm just looking at it.

This is a quick and easy quilt to create and would be a perfect design for someone who has never made a jelly roll quilt before and 'just wants to get started'. The design echoes the antique quilt and its piecing couldn't be easier. It could be quilted in your favourite way, by hand or machine. The quilt was made by the authors and longarm quilted by The Quilt Room.

Sweet Sixteen Quilt

Vital Statistics

Finished Size: 72in x 72in
Block Size: 8in square
Number of Blocks: 81
Setting: 9 x 9 blocks

Requirements

- One jelly roll **OR** forty 2½in wide strips cut across the width of the fabric
- 2¾yd (2.5m) of background fabric
- 24in (60cm) of fabric for binding

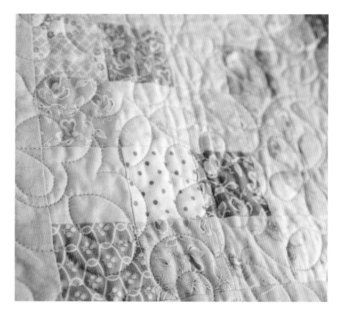

CUTTING INSTRUCTIONS

JELLY ROLL STRIPS:

- Cut each jelly roll strip in half to create eighty half strips 2½in x 21in approximately.

BACKGROUND FABRIC:

- Cut eleven 8½in wide strips across the width of the fabric and subcut each into four 8½in squares. You need forty-one in total, so three are spare.

BINDING FABRIC:

- Cut eight 2½in wide strips across the width of the fabric.

MAKING THE SIXTEEN-PATCH BLOCKS

1 Select four jelly roll half strips and sew them together lengthways as in the diagram below. Press the seams in one direction. Your strip unit should measure 8½in wide so adjust your seam allowance if your unit doesn't match this measurement.

2 Lay one strip unit on the cutting mat at a time. Trim the selvedge and subcut into eight 2½in segments. Always line up the markings on the ruler with the seam to make sure you are cutting at a right angle.

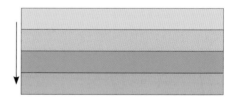

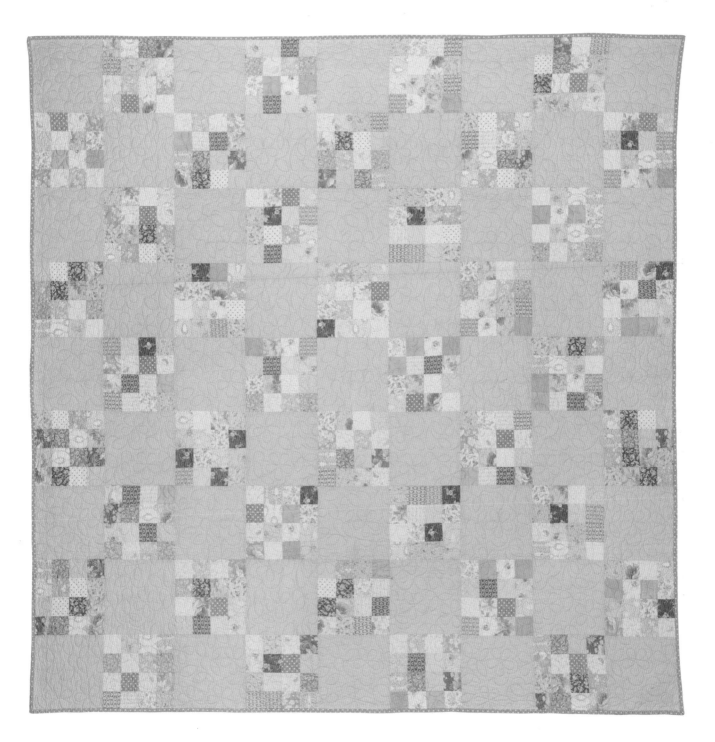

3 Repeat steps 1 and 2 to make twenty strip units and subcut each into eight 2½in segments. You need 160 2½in segments in total.

4 Choose four different segments and sew them together, turning alternate segments around so the seams are in opposite directions. Pin at every seam intersection to ensure a perfect match. Try not to sew squares of the same fabric next to each other. Press the finished block.

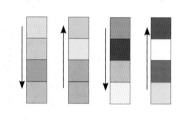

5 Repeat the process to make forty sixteen-patch blocks in total.

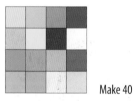

Make 40

ASSEMBLING THE QUILT

6 Lay out the blocks as shown in the diagram, alternating a sixteen-patch block with a background square. Sew the blocks into rows, pressing the seams towards the background square. Sew the rows together, pinning at every seam intersection to ensure a perfect match and then press.

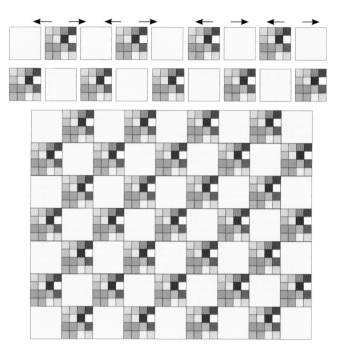

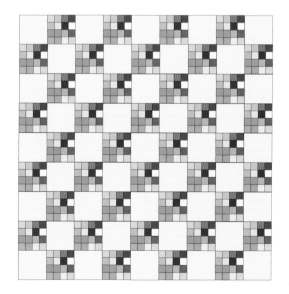

FINISHING THE QUILT

7 The quilt top is now complete. Prepare the top, wadding (batting) and backing fabric for quilting and quilt as desired – see Quilting in the General Techniques section. Bind the quilt to finish, following the instructions in Binding a Quilt.

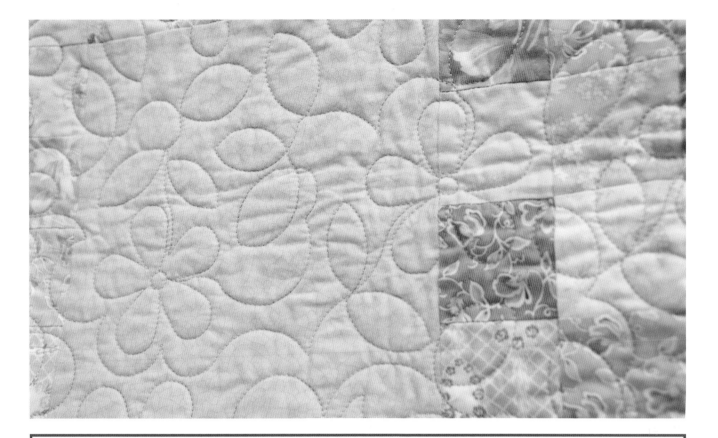

Heirloom Quilt Ideas

Sixteen-patch blocks are perfect for using up scraps from your stash but you can also create patterns with them by more careful colour arrangement.

For example, try creating a diagonal pattern across the quilt by using very dark-coloured squares through the diagonal of each block.

The background fabric could be changed to a much darker colour, so the plain squares have more drama. You could feature motif quilting in these squares.

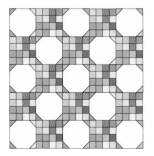

Instead of using plain squares you could use other blocks, such as the snowball block shown in this final layout diagram.

JEWEL IN THE CROWN

Antique Inspiration

This is an American Depression-era quilt dating to around the 1930s. Its charming but simple layout is created with machine piecing and its existence may well be due to the entrepreneurial efforts of an American called Isaac Merritt Singer. We have to thank Mr Singer for the fact that so many families had sewing machines by the 1930s. He started the Singer Manufacturing Company in 1865 and came up with the clever idea of allowing families to buy sewing machines by spreading the cost on an instalment plan. This made buying a machine much more affordable to families, particularly those suffering from the economic downturn, and by 1870 the sewing machine had become available to all women, not just the wealthy.

This quilt is a single Irish Chain design with a pretty scalloped edge. The nine-patch blocks alternate with plain squares, making it easy to piece by machine. It is very finely hand quilted with a grid pattern in the nine-patch blocks and filled in with a tulip quilting design and a tulip border. The quilt measures 70in x 87in (178cm x 221cm).

Today's Heirloom

For our heirloom quilt we decided to use a jelly roll of reproduction 1930s fabrics, combined with a white-on-white fabric for the background. During the 1920s colour tastes were changing and although women still admired the darker, traditional shades they began to seek out lighter, brighter colours. A fresh, pastel look became popular and this is the one we have tried to create with our modern-day interpretation. This cozy and welcoming quilt is so easy to put together and would be perfect for many different décors.

Embroidery experienced a revival in the early 20th century and skilled hand work was often incorporated into quilts. We couldn't match the exquisite hand quilting in our antique quilt so we chose to longarm quilt a 1930s flower design, which we felt was appropriate. The quilt was made by the authors and longarm quilted by The Quilt Room.

Jewel in the Crown Quilt

Vital Statistics

Finished Size: 69in x 87in
Block Size: 6in square
Number of Blocks: 80 nine-patch blocks and 63 background squares
Setting: On point

Requirements

- One jelly roll **OR** forty 2½in strips cut across the width of the fabric
- 4½yd (4.10m) of background fabric
- Jelly roll strips are used for the binding

SORTING YOUR STRIPS

- Choose twenty-five jelly roll strips for the blocks.
- Choose eight jelly roll strips for the binding.
- Seven are spare.

CUTTING INSTRUCTIONS

BACKGROUND FABRIC:

- Cut eleven 6½in wide strips and subcut each into six 6½in squares. You need sixty-three squares in total.
- Cut twenty 2½in wide strips for the nine-patch blocks.
- Cut two strips 10in wide and subcut each strip into four 10in squares. Cut across both diagonals to form thirty-two setting triangles.
- Cut one 5½in strip and subcut into two 5½in squares. Cut across one diagonal to form four corner triangles. Cutting the setting and corner triangles this way ensures the outer edges of your quilt are not on the bias. You need thirty-two setting triangles and four corner triangles.

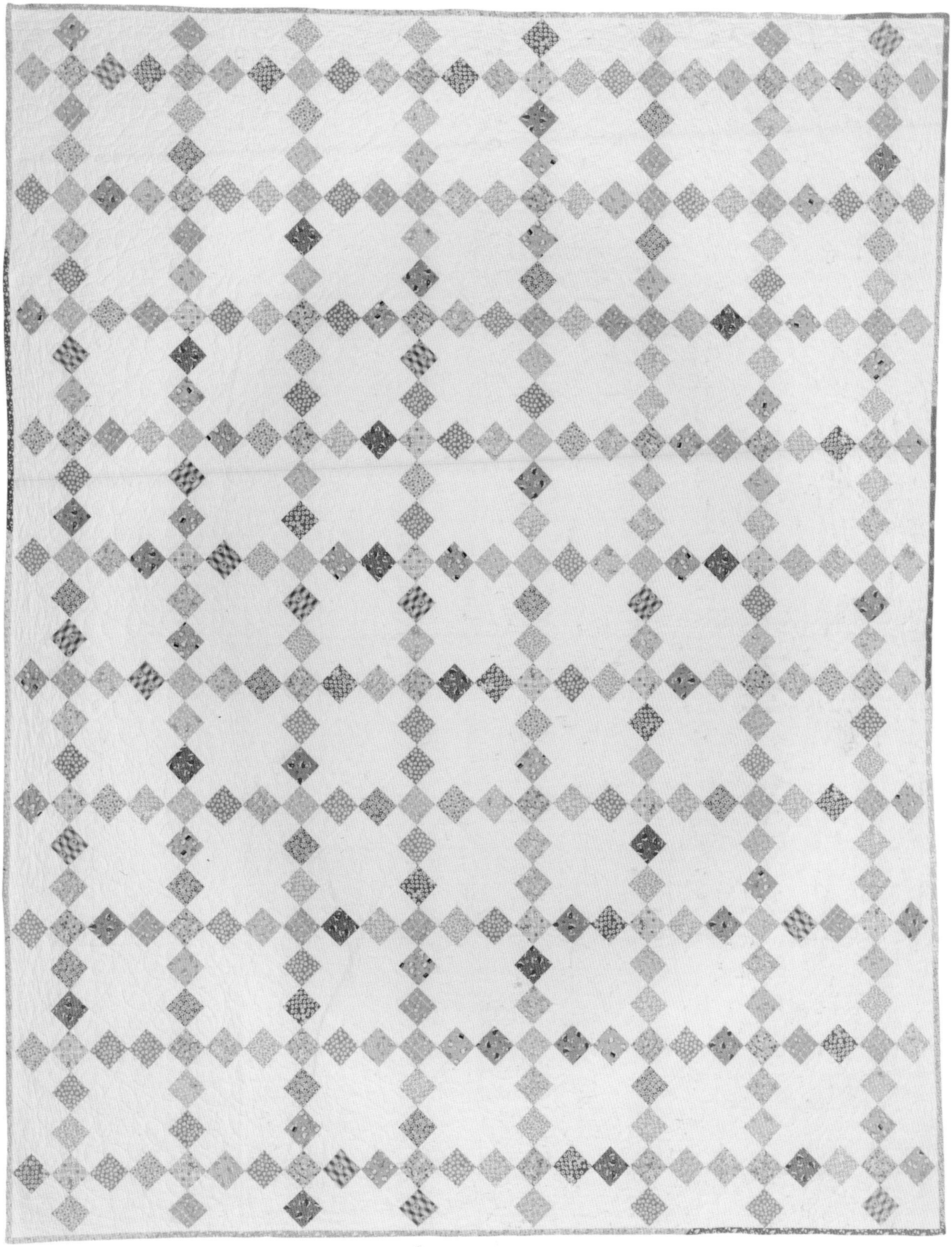

MAKING THE NINE-PATCH BLOCKS

1 Using the jelly roll strips allocated for the blocks, sew a jelly roll strip to both sides of a 2½in background strip as shown in the diagram below to make Unit A. Repeat to make ten Unit As. Press seams in the directions shown.

Unit A

2 Subcut each Unit A into sixteen 2½in segments. You need 160 in total.

3 Sew a 2½in background strip to both sides of a jelly roll strip as shown in the diagram to make Unit B. Repeat to make five Unit Bs. Press seams as shown.

Unit B

4 Sub-cut each Unit B into sixteen 2½in segments. You need eighty in total.

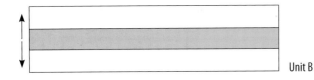

5 Choose two segments from Unit A and one segment from Unit B. Sew the segments together as shown to create a nine-patch block, pinning at every seam intersection to ensure a perfect match. Your blocks can be as scrappy as you like. Repeat to make eighty nine-patch blocks.

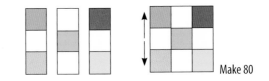

Make 80

SETTING THE BLOCKS ON POINT

6 Create Row 1 by sewing a setting triangle to both sides of a nine-patch block as shown in the diagram. The setting triangles have been cut slightly larger to make the blocks 'float', so when sewing the setting triangles make sure the bottom of the triangle is aligned with the block. Press as shown.

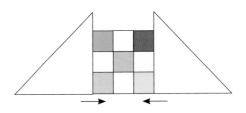

7 Create Row 2 by sewing a setting triangle to each side of a nine-patch block with a background 6½in square in the centre. Press towards the nine-patch blocks.

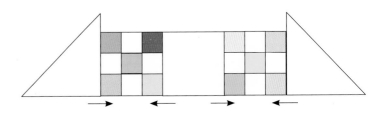

8 Following the quilt diagram, right, continue to sew the blocks together to form rows, alternating the nine-patch blocks and the background squares and sewing a setting triangle to each end. Pin at every intersection to ensure a perfect match.

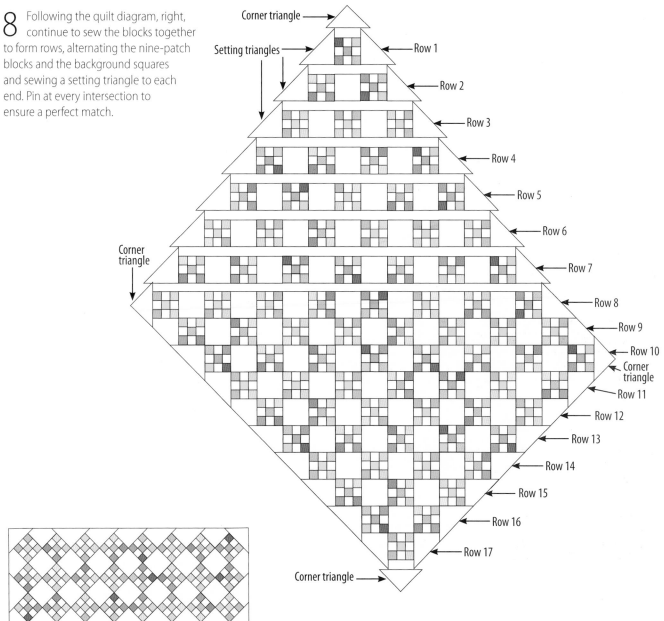

Corner triangle

Setting triangles

Row 1
Row 2
Row 3
Row 4
Row 5
Row 6
Row 7
Row 8
Row 9
Row 10
Corner triangle
Row 11
Row 12
Row 13
Row 14
Row 15
Row 16
Row 17

Corner triangle

Corner triangle

9 Now sew the rows together, pinning at every intersection. Sew the corner triangles on last and trim them to size if necessary.

FINISHING THE QUILT

10 The quilt top is now complete. Prepare the top, wadding (batting) and backing fabric for quilting and quilt as desired – see Quilting in General Techniques. Bind the quilt to finish, following the instructions in Binding a Quilt.

To make a scrappy binding take the eight jelly roll strips allocated for the binding and cut each into four rectangles approximately 2½in x 10½in. Sew them into a continuous length, trying not to have two rectangles of the same fabric next to each other.

CHAIN REACTION

Antique Inspiration

This wonderful quilt was made in America during the 1930s. It uses a triple Irish Chain layout made with 1in squares and is totally hand sewn and hand quilted – even the calico background was cut into 1in squares and sewn together! It certainly is a labour of love. This antique quilt measures 72in x 92in (183cm x 234cm).

Quilt making was undergoing a major resurgence during the 1930s. In 1933 the World's Fair was held in Chicago, USA to celebrate the city's 100th anniversary and a century of progress. It has been estimated that an amazing twenty million people attended this fair. As part of the event Sears, Roebuck and Company, America's largest retailer at the time, sponsored the Sears National Quilt Contest, offering total prize money of $7,500. This was an enormous sum of money, especially during a time of recession, and not surprisingly they had 25,000 entrants. The winning quilt was called Star of the Bluegrass and was awarded $1,000 prize money. Having judged the Jelly Roll Dream Challenge we find it hard to imagine the enormity of this event and it shows just how popular quilting was during this time, despite the terrible economic conditions.

Today's Heirloom

The antique quilt was our inspiration but for our modern heirloom we decided that while honouring the design layout of the original quilt we would choose a totally different colour plan. We wanted to use the vibrant colours and extrovert patterns of designer Kaffe Fassett and these fabrics just called out for a dark background to emphasize them. The result is a bold and striking creation that would work well with many contemporary interiors.

Working with the jelly roll, our squares increased to 2in and we decided that our background fabric really didn't need to be cut into 2in squares as they could be created from variously sized larger rectangles. The quilt went together very easily and was quick and simple to sew together thanks to some clever strip piecing. The quilt was made by the authors and longarm quilted by The Quilt Room.

Chain Reaction Quilt

Vital Statistics

Finished Size: 76in x 76in
Block Size: 12in square
Number of Blocks: 36
Setting: 6 x 6 blocks plus 2in border

Requirements

- One jelly roll **OR** forty 2½in wide strips cut across the width of the fabric
- 2¾yd (2.5m) of fabric for the background and the border
- 1½yd (1.4m) of accent fabric
- 24in (60cm) of binding fabric

CUTTING INSTRUCTIONS

JELLY ROLL STRIPS:

- Cut all forty jelly roll strips in half to create eighty rectangles measuring 2½in x 22in approximately.

ACCENT FABRIC:

- Cut twenty 2½in strips across the width of the fabric and cut each in half to create forty rectangles approximately 2½in x 22in.

BACKGROUND FABRIC:

- Cut thirteen strips 2½in wide across the fabric width.
  - Set eight aside for the borders.
  - Cut the remaining five in half to create ten rectangles approximately 2½in x 22in.
- Cut five 4½in strips across the width of the fabric and cut each in half to create ten rectangles approximately 4½in x 22in.
- Cut five 6½in wide strips across the fabric width and cut each in half to create ten rectangles approximately 6½in x 22in.

BINDING FABRIC:

- Cut eight 2½in wide strips across the width of the fabric.

SORTING THE STRIPS

- After cutting your fabrics, make five separate piles as follows.
  - Eighty jelly roll rectangles.
  - Forty accent rectangles.
  - Ten 2½in wide background rectangles.
  - Ten 4½in background rectangles.
  - Ten 6½in background rectangles.

SEWING STRIP UNIT A

1 You now need to make three different Strip Units – Strip Unit A, Strip Unit B and Strip Unit C, as follows. For Strip Unit A choose three jelly roll rectangles, two accent rectangles and one 2½in background rectangle and sew them into Strip Unit A as shown in the diagram below. Do not spend too much time on your selection. A good policy is to use what is next in the pile unless it is just too similar. Press the seams as shown. Repeat to create a total of ten Strip Unit As.

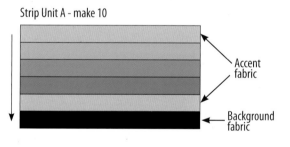

Strip Unit A - make 10

Accent fabric

Background fabric

2 Lay one Strip Unit A on the cutting mat at a time. Trim the selvedge and subcut into eight 2½in segments. Always line up the markings on the ruler with the seams to make sure you are cutting at a right angle. Cut eighty Unit A segments.

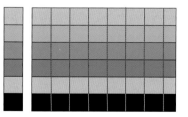

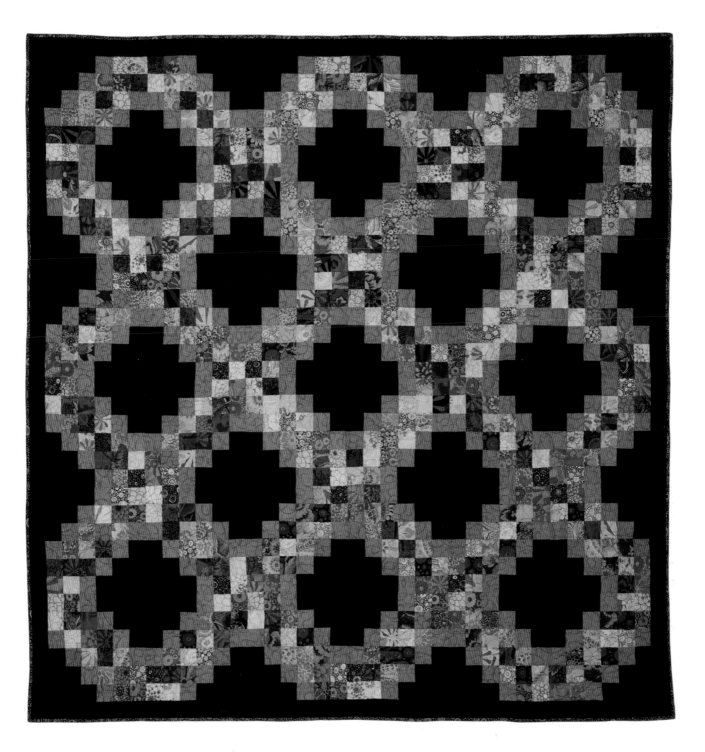

SEWING STRIP UNIT B

3 Choose three jelly roll rectangles, one accent rectangle and one 4½in background rectangle and sew them into Strip Unit B. Press seams as shown in the diagram. Repeat to create a total of ten Strip Unit Bs.

Strip Unit B - make 10

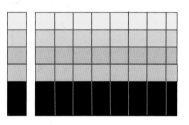

← Accent

← Background

4 Lay one Strip Unit B on the cutting mat at a time. Trim the selvedge and subcut into eight 2½in wide segments in the same way as you did for Strip Unit A. Cut eighty Unit B segments.

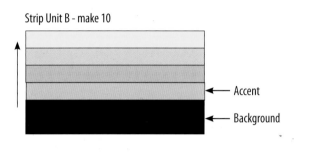

SEWING STRIP UNIT C

5 Choose two jelly roll rectangles, one accent rectangle and one 6½in background rectangle and sew them into Strip Unit C. Press seams as shown. Repeat to create a total of ten Strip Unit Cs.

Strip Unit C - make 10

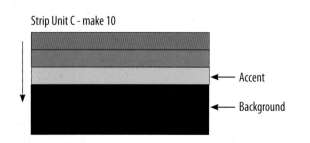

← Accent

← Background

6 Lay one Strip Unit C on the cutting mat at a time. Trim the selvedge and subcut into eight 2½in segments, just as you did for Strip Units A and B. Cut eighty Unit C segments.

7 Put the Unit A, Unit B and Unit C segments into three piles, making sure that the background fabric always faces the same way.

Unit A   Unit B   Unit C

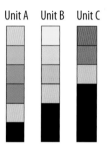

SEWING THE BLOCKS

8 Choose one Unit A, one Unit B and one Unit C and sew together as shown in the diagram, pinning at every seam intersection to ensure a perfect match. The seams will nest together nicely. Try to have different fabrics next to each other. Repeat to make eighty units like this. Press seams towards Unit C as shown. Seventy-two units are needed for the quilt. The extra eight units will make four blocks, which could be used to create a coordinating cushion.

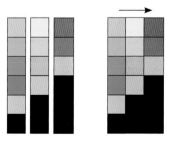

9 Choose two of these units and rotate one of the units 180 degrees. Sew together as shown, pinning at every seam intersection to ensure a perfect match and then press. Repeat to make thirty-six blocks for the quilt. You could make up the extra four blocks at this stage if you like.

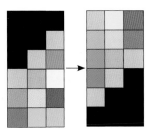

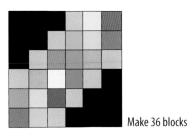

Make 36 blocks

ASSEMBLING THE QUILT

10 Referring to the diagram below, lay out the blocks into six rows of six blocks each, rotating alternate blocks 90 degrees. When you are happy with the layout, sew the blocks into rows and then sew the rows together, pinning at every seam intersection to ensure a perfect match

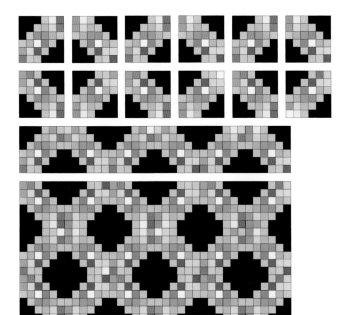

11 Join the border strips into a continuous length. Determine the vertical measurement from top to bottom through the centre of your quilt top. Cut two side borders to this measurement. Pin and sew to the quilt and press.

12 Now determine the horizontal measurement from side to side across the centre of the quilt top. Cut two borders to this measurement. Sew to the top and bottom of your quilt and press.

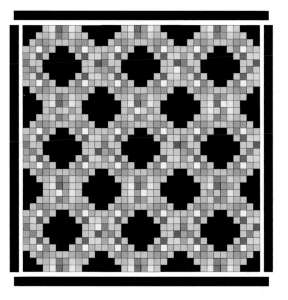

FINISHING THE QUILT

13 The quilt top is now complete. Prepare the top, wadding (batting) and backing fabric for quilting and quilt as desired – see Quilting in General Techniques. Bind the quilt to finish, following the instructions in Binding a Quilt.

BEAUTIFUL BOW TIES

Antique Inspiration

This gorgeous American quilt dates from the 1940s, although some of the fabrics are probably a little earlier. During the late 1930s and early 1940s quilting on both sides of the Atlantic took a back seat to the spectre and then the reality of war on a worldwide scale. Understandably, women's attention was focused elsewhere although quilts were still made of course, often on a patriotic theme. Popular patterns used in quilts of this time included Delectable Mountains, Feathered Star, Double Wedding Ring and Bow Tie, the pattern used in this antique quilt. In fact, the Bow Tie or Necktie block has an amazing number of variations.

This quilt has the most fabulous collection of fabrics, including checks, spots and stripes in blues, reds, whites, greys and tans. The individual bow tie blocks are hand pieced and the blocks are then sewn together by sewing machine. It is hand quilted with a plain cotton backing and a cotton wadding (batting). The quilt measures 75in x 82in (191cm x 208cm).

Today's Heirloom

Sometimes you can find the perfect jelly roll for a project and this is exactly what we felt about the range we used in this quilt. American Banner Rose by Minick & Simpson had just the right colouring and combined with some Lecien fabric, which we used for our background fabric, it created a lovely antique-looking quilt.

To create a scrappier look to our quilt we used two different background fabrics instead of just one, totalling 2 yards (1.75 metres). The bow tie blocks stand out well against the background fabric and we also added a border to our modern version to increase its overall size and make it into a useful bed-sized quilt. The quilt was made by the authors and longarm quilted by The Quilt Room.

Beautiful Bow Ties Quilt

Vital Statistics

Finished Size: 56in x 56in
Block Size: 4in square
Number of Blocks: 196
Setting: 14 x 14 blocks plus 3in border

Requirements

- One jelly roll **OR** forty 2½in wide strips cut across the width of the fabric
- 2yd (1.75m) of background fabric or if you prefer a scrappy background use different fabrics totalling 2yd (1.75m) – we used two background fabrics in our quilt
- 24in (60cm) of border fabric
- 20in (50cm) of binding fabric

SORTING AND CUTTING YOUR FABRICS

JELLY ROLL STRIPS:

- Cut each of the forty jelly roll strips as follows:
  – Cut ten 2½in squares.
  – Take the remainder of the strip (which measures approximately 2½in x 17in) and trim to measure 1½in x 17in. Subcut into ten 1½in x 1½in squares.
- Keep the 2½in squares and 1½in squares from each jelly roll strip together in one pile. Each jelly roll strip will make five bow tie blocks.

BACKGROUND FABRIC:

- Cut twenty-five 2½in wide strips across the width of the fabric. Subcut each strip into sixteen 2½in x 2½in squares. You need 392 in total – you will have eight spare.

BORDER FABRIC:

- Cut six 3½in wide strips across the width of the fabric.

BINDING FABRIC:

- Cut six 2½in wide strips across the width of the fabric.

MAKING THE BOW TIE BLOCKS

1 Working with one pile of jelly roll squares at a time, mark a diagonal line from corner to corner on the wrong side of a 1½in square as shown in the diagram below.

2 With right sides together, lay a marked square on one corner of a 2½in background square, aligning the outer edges. Sew across the diagonal, using the marked diagonal line as the stitching line. After a while you may find you do not need to draw the line as it is not difficult to judge the sewing line. An alternative is to fold the square and use the fold to guide you.

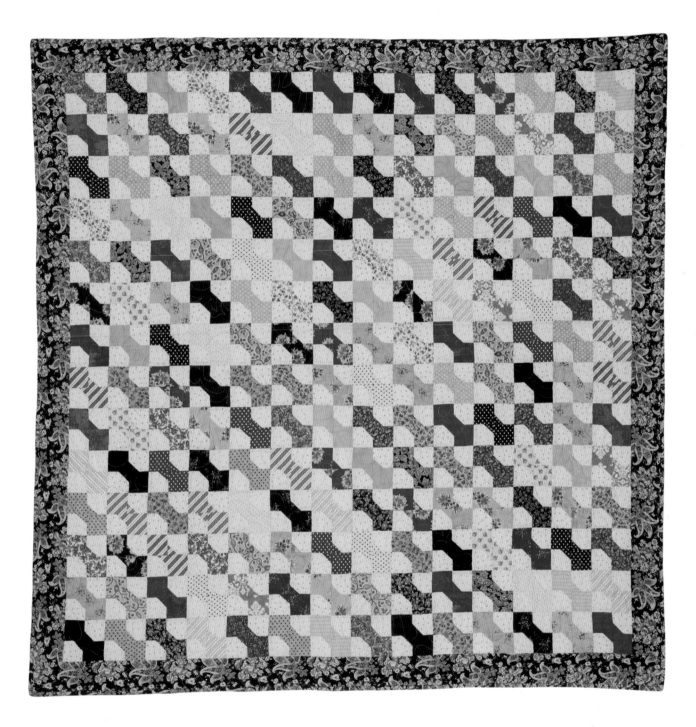

3 Flip the jelly roll square over and press towards the outside of the block. Trim excess fabric from the jelly roll square but do not trim the background fabric, as this will help keep the patchwork in shape. Repeat to make two units.

4 Take the two units and two 2½in jelly roll squares and sew together as shown, pinning at the seam intersection to ensure a perfect match. Press the seams towards the jelly roll squares and your seams will nest together nicely.

5 Repeat to make five bow tie blocks from each pile of jelly roll squares. You need 196 blocks in total.

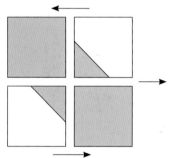

ASSEMBLING THE QUILT

6 Lay out your blocks into fourteen rows of fourteen blocks. When you are happy with the layout, sew fourteen blocks together to form one row. Repeat this to make fourteen rows. Press the seams of alternate rows in opposite directions so that the seams will nest together nicely when sewn together.

7 Now sew the rows together, pinning at every seam intersection to ensure a perfect match.

ADDING THE BORDER

8 Join the border strips into a continuous length. Determine the vertical measurement from top to bottom through the centre of your quilt top. Cut two side borders to this measurement. Pin and sew to the quilt and press.

9 Determine the horizontal measurement from side to side across the centre of the quilt top. Cut two borders to this measurement. Sew to the top and bottom of your quilt and press.

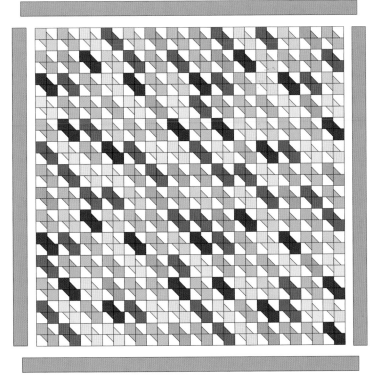

FINISHING THE QUILT

10 The quilt top is now complete. Prepare the top, wadding (batting) and backing fabric for quilting and quilt as desired – see Quilting in General Techniques. Bind the quilt to finish, following the instructions in Binding a Quilt.

Heirloom Quilt Ideas

To create a completely different pattern with the bow tie blocks, try rotating every other block 90 degrees, to form a linked circles effect.

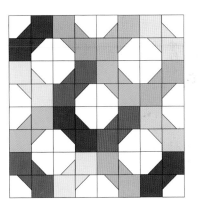

The bow tie blocks could also be alternated with a different block, perhaps by repeating the triangle unit from the bow tie block to create a square on point within a square.

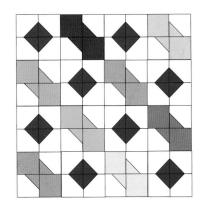

NORTH BY NORTHWEST

Antique Inspiration

This is an American quilt and dates from the late 19th century. The pattern is a variation of a sawtooth square design and features a wonderful array of stunning fabrics. The earthy tones give it a comfortable country look, especially with the green shades that have been used. In the 18th century fabrics were usually dyed with vegetable dyes made from roots, bark, herbs and flowers, which create rich, earthy tones, but the 19th century brought vast improvements in dye manufacture and aniline dyes made from synthetic compounds expanded the colour palette immensely. At the time this quilt was sewn the small pieces would have made it an ideal quilt to create from fabric scraps and old clothing.

This quilt was bought as a quilt top and it was longarm quilted before being given as a present to a very special friend, Lally Long. Thanks to Lally for allowing us to borrow it back. The quilt measures 75in x 75in (191cm x 191cm).

Today's Heirloom

For our heirloom quilt we wanted to capture the same look as the antique quilt and so we used an Antique Fair jelly roll designed by Blackbird Designs, which had just the right combination of colours, including the earthy tones we so admired in the original. A cream-on-cream background fabric was selected to set off all the lovely colours.

Sawtooth patterns in quilt making have been around for centuries and make bold geometric statements, especially when strongly contrasting dark and light fabrics are used for the half-square triangles. Many distinctive quilt blocks can be created with half-square triangles, including Sawtooth Star, Bear's Paw and Delectable Mountains. This quilt uses two alternating blocks – one composed just from half-square triangles and the other from half-square triangles on two sides of a plain square. The quilt was made by the authors and longarm quilted by The Quilt Room.

North by Northwest Quilt

Vital Statistics

Finished Size: 68in x 68in
Block Size: 6in square
Number of Blocks: 121
Setting: 11 x 11 blocks plus 2in border on two sides

Requirements

- One jelly roll **OR** forty 2½in wide strips cut across the width of the fabric
- 3½yd (3.25m) of background fabric
- 24in (60cm) of binding fabric
- Multi-Size 45/90 or other speciality ruler for cutting half-square triangles from strips

SORTING YOUR STRIPS

- There is no sorting of strips. They will all be used randomly in the half-square triangle units.

CUTTING INSTRUCTIONS

BACKGROUND FABRIC:

- Cut four 4½in wide strips across the width of the fabric.
- Cut forty 2½in wide strips across the width of the fabric.

BINDING FABRIC:

- Cut eight 2½in strips across the width of the fabric.

MAKING THE HALF-SQUARE TRIANGLES

1 There is very little wastage in this quilt so take care not to trim selvedges too much. Take a jelly roll strip and a 2½in background strip and press right sides together ensuring that they are exactly one on top of the other. The pressing will help hold the two strips together.

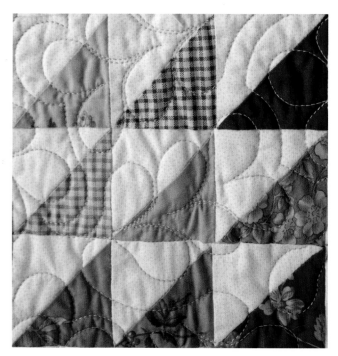

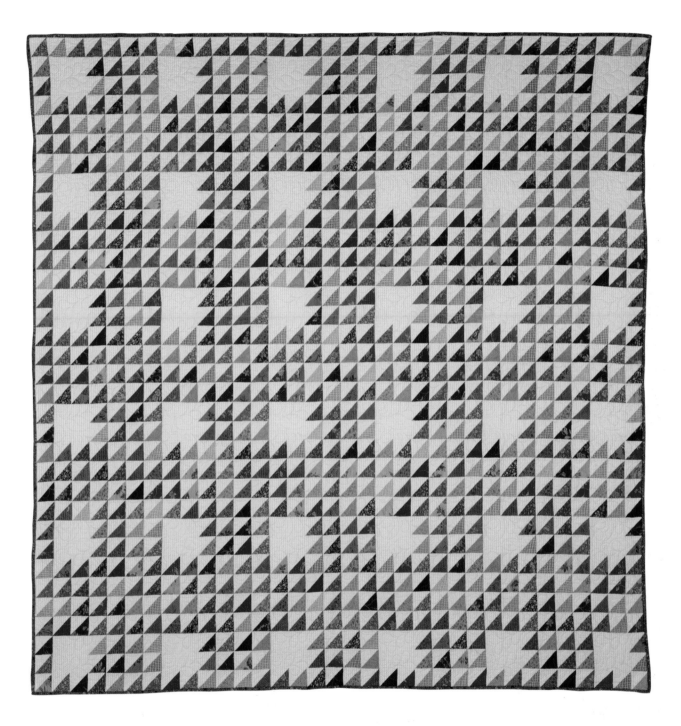

2 Lay the pressed strips on a cutting mat and position the Multi-Size 45/90 ruler as shown in the diagram, lining up the 2in mark at the bottom edge of the strips. Trim the selvedge and cut the first triangle. You will notice that the cut out triangle has a flat top. This would just have been a dog ear you needed to cut off so it is saving you time.

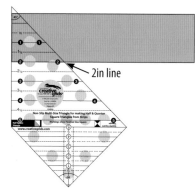

3 Rotate the ruler 180 degrees as shown and cut the next triangle. Continue along the strip cutting the required amount of triangles. Cut twenty-six triangles from each strip.

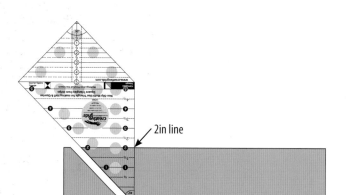

4 Sew along the diagonal of each pair of triangles. Trim the dog ears and press open towards the jelly roll fabric to form twenty-six half-square triangle units.

5 Repeat with all forty jelly roll strips to make 1,040 in total. The blocks will use 945, sixty-seven are used in the borders and twenty-eight are spare. Yes, it sounds a lot but chain piecing speeds things up immensely, and don't forget that this is an heirloom quilt!

SEWING ROW A

6 Sew two half-square triangle units together as shown. Press and sew to the right-hand side of a 4½in background square. Press as shown.

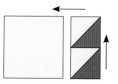

7 Sew three half-square triangle units together as shown and sew to the bottom of a 4½in background square that has the two half-square triangles attached. This is Block A1. Repeat to make thirty-six of Block A1.

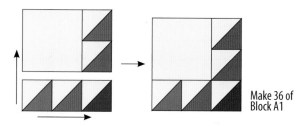

Make 36 of Block A1

8 Sew three sets of three half-square triangle units together and press as shown. Sew the rows together to form Block A2. Repeat to make thirty of Block A2.

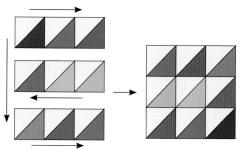

Make 30 of Block A2

9 Sew together six Block A1s alternating with five Block A2s to create Row A. Pin at every seam intersection to ensure a perfect match. Repeat to create six of these rows, pressing as shown.

Row A - make 6

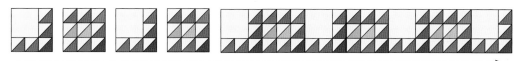

SEWING ROW B

10 Sew three sets of three half-square triangle units together and press as shown. Sew the rows together to form Block B. Repeat to make fifty-five Block B. *Note*: the only difference between Block A2 and Block B is the direction in which you press the seams. Pressing in the correct direction will really help when piecing the rows together. Press thirty of Block B *downwards* and twenty-five blocks *upwards*, as shown in the diagram.

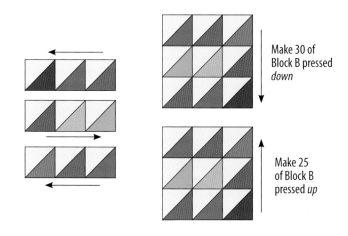

Make 30 of
Block B pressed
down

Make 25
of Block B
pressed *up*

11 Sew together eleven Block Bs to create Row B, alternating the blocks pressed in different directions. Pin at seam intersections to ensure a perfect match. Repeat to create five rows, pressing as shown.

Row B - make 5

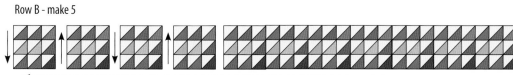

ASSEMBLING THE QUILT

12 Referring to the diagram below lay out the rows, alternating Rows A and B and when you are happy with the arrangement sew the rows together pinning at every seam intersection to ensure a perfect match.

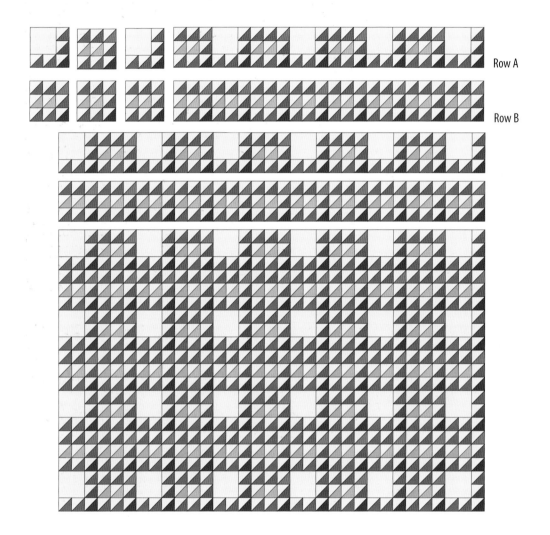

Row A

Row B

ADDING THE BORDER

13 A border is only required on the left side of the quilt and along the top. Sew thirty-three half-square triangle units together as shown. Now sew thirty-four half-square triangle units together as shown.

Left side border

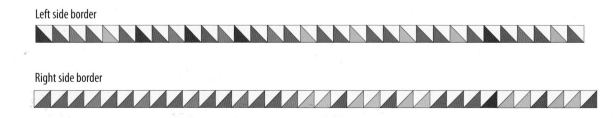

Right side border

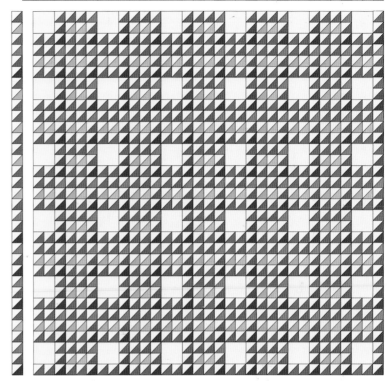

14 Take the thirty-three half-square triangles border and sew it to the left-hand side of the quilt. Press seams outwards. Sew the remaining border to the top of the quilt.

FINISHING THE QUILT
15 The quilt top is now complete. Prepare the top, wadding (batting) and backing fabric for quilting and quilt as desired – see Quilting in General Techniques. Bind the quilt to finish, following the instructions in Binding a Quilt.

PYRAMID TRIANGLES

Antique Inspiration

This is an American quilt dating back to the 1930s – the time of the Great Depression, a period of severe worldwide economic depression. During this difficult time, which lasted around ten years, women were making the family clothes in order to save money and the scraps from making clothes were saved and used to make quilts. Magazines too were trying to survive and they did this by selling fashion and optimism. To achieve this new quilt patterns were included in each edition, as quilting was one activity where women could be creative whilst doing something useful for their families. During the Depression there was a real quilt revival and the quilts from that period are known as Depression quilts.

   This quilt has been loved and much used over its long life. It has obviously been washed many times and with its thin cotton wadding and hand quilting its feel is soft and welcoming. The colouring used for the sashing is sunny and bright and the quilt must have brought a little sunshine into any home it was used in. The quilt measures 82½in x 66½in (209cm x 169cm).

Today's Heirloom

The fresh and bright colours of the antique quilt are echoed here in our modern interpretation, including the white background and the sunny sashing. Using a jelly roll was just perfect for making all the small quarter-square and half-square triangles in the blocks and absolutely nothing was wasted. We are always pleased when we can use up every scrap of fabric – just as a thrifty 1930s housewife would have been. We used a jelly roll by Moda called Oasis by Three Sisters, which has lovely shades of peach, cream, lemon and dusky blue.

For our sashing and border we chose a marble dot in a slightly paler shade of yellow and we hope you agree that it looks lovely, yet still very true to the original inspiration. After adding the background and sashing fabric we ended up with a very nice double-bed size quilt but the design would be easy to scale down to a smaller quilt if desired.

Pyramid Triangles Quilt

Vital Statistics

Finished Size: 78in x 93in
Block Size: 12in square
Number of Blocks: 30
Setting: 5 blocks x 6 blocks plus 3in sashing and borders

Requirements

- One jelly roll **OR** forty 2½in strips cut across the width of the fabric
- 2¼yd (2m) of background fabric
- 2½yd (2.25m) of sashing fabric
- ¾yd (65cm) of binding fabric
- Multi-Size 45/90 triangle or other specialist ruler for cutting quarter-square triangles

SORTING THE STRIPS

- Divide the jelly roll into the following strips.
  – Nine light strips.
  – Thirty-one medium strips.

CUTTING INSTRUCTIONS

JELLY ROLL STRIPS:

- Keep each strip folded double when cutting so that two triangles are cut at the same time. This makes it easier when piecing the blocks as each block requires two each of a triangle from the same fabric.
- Using the following technique, cut each folded jelly roll strip into fourteen quarter-square triangles. From the nine light strips you get 126 light quarter-square triangles (six are spare) and from the thirty-one medium strips you get 434 medium quarter-square triangles (fourteen are spare). Keep the light triangles in a separate pile. For speed you can layer more than one folded strip but take care not to lose accuracy.
- Position the Multi-Size 45/90 ruler on the strip as shown in the first diagram, lining up the 4in marker line with the bottom of the strip. Cut either side of the ruler to form one quarter-square triangle.

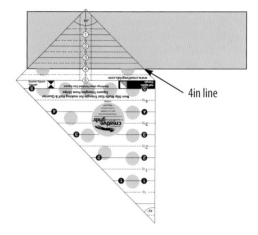

4in line

- Now rotate the ruler 180 degrees and cut another triangle. Continue along the folded strip to cut seven triangles, which will produce fourteen quarter-square triangles.

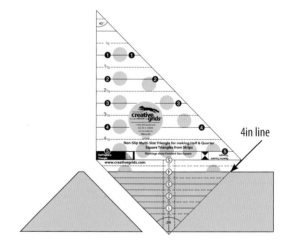

4in line

BACKGROUND FABRIC:

- Cut ten 7in wide strips across the width of the fabric.
  – Subcut each strip into six 7in squares to make sixty squares.
  – Cut cross the diagonal of each square to form 120 half-square triangles.

SASHING FABRIC:

- Cut two 3½in wide strips across the width of the fabric.
  - Subcut each into three rectangles 3½in x 12½in, to make six in total.
- Refold the balance of the fabric lengthways and cut twelve 3½in wide strips lengthways down the fabric.
  - Leave seven for the horizontal sashing to be trimmed to size later.
  - Take five strips and subcut each strip into six rectangles 3½in x 12½in. Add these to the six already cut. You need thirty-six in total.

BINDING:

- Cut nine 2½in wide strips across the width of the fabric.

MAKING THE BLOCKS

1 Take two light triangles of the same fabric and two medium triangles of the same fabric and sew two units as shown in the diagram below. Trim dog ears and press towards the medium triangles.

2 With right sides together, sew the two units together pinning at the centre seam intersection to ensure a perfect match. Press the work.

3 Take two medium triangles of one fabric and two medium triangles of another fabric and sew together as shown. Note that the fabrics for these triangles change position. Trim dog ears and press towards the darker triangle.

4 Sew these units to both sides of the quarter-square triangle unit, as shown. Press in the directions shown.

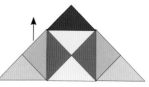

5 Sew one medium triangle to the top. Press as shown and then trim all dog ears. The other triangle in the pair can be used in another unit.

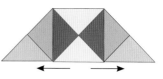

6 Sew a background half-square triangle to both sides of the unit and press towards the background fabric. Press as indicated on the diagram.

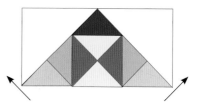

7 Repeat steps 1 to 6 – you will need to make sixty triangle units in total.

ASSEMBLING THE QUILT

8 Pair up the triangle units and sew the pairs together to form thirty blocks. Using a large quilting square, at least 12½in, check the measurement of your block and trim to 12½in square if necessary.

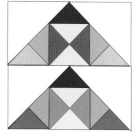

Make 30

ADDING THE SASHING AND BORDER STRIPS

9 Add the vertical sashing as follows. Sew a 3½in x 12½in sashing strip to the left side and the right side of one block and to the right side only of four blocks, as shown.

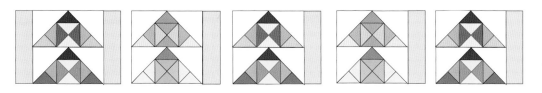

10 Sew the blocks together to form one row. Press towards the sashing strips. Repeat to make six rows in total.

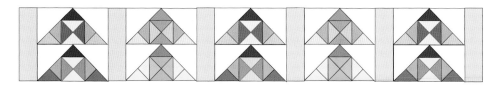

11 Add the horizontal sashing as follows. Measure the width of the rows and trim all the horizontal sashing strips to the same size. It is important that they are all trimmed to the same size in order to keep the quilt square.

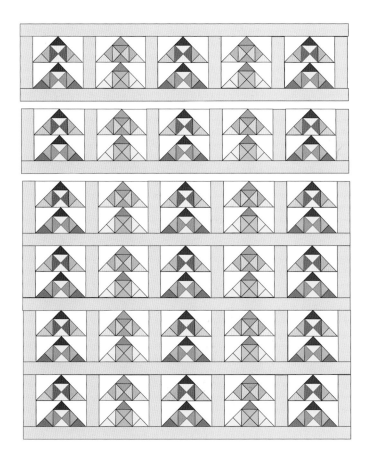

12 Sew a horizontal sashing strip to the top and bottom of the first row and to the bottom of the other five rows. When joining the sashing to a row, mark the centre of both the sashing strip and the row and pin in position. Now pin at both ends and continue pinning in position, easing if necessary. Sew the rows together.

13 Your quilt top is now complete. Prepare the top, wadding (batting) and backing fabric for quilting and then quilt as desired – see Quilting in General Techniques. Bind the quilt to finish, following the instructions in Binding a Quilt.

IN THE LOG HOUSE

Antique Inspiration

The log cabin quilt design is instantly recognizable and has been a popular pattern on both sides of the Atlantic for countless years. This quilt, which belongs to Pam's husband (yes, he has been totally indoctrinated into the quilting world!), is a Victorian example made from a stunning array of fabrics. At a glance you can see silk, satin, velvet, taffeta and many tartans. In 1855 the rebuilding of Balmoral Castle, the home of the British Royal Family in Scotland, rekindled an interest in all things Scottish and this quilt includes many plaid and tartan fabrics, placing its date to after that time. Silks of that period were sometimes artificially weighted, to make them rustle and give the impression of quality and luxury. Unfortunately, the process eventually leads to the fabrics disintegrating and this has happened to a number of the gorgeous silks in this quilt, although luckily not too many.

Early log cabin blocks were almost always pieced on to foundation fabric and this quilt is no exception. The scraps of fabric were hand pieced on to a fabric foundation and then the blocks were machine sewn together. The sewing machine was becoming more and more popular by the end of the 19th century and we believe this quilt dates to around that time. The quilt measures 71in x 61in (180cm x 155cm).

Today's Heirloom

Inspired by the design and colours of the antique quilt we have created this quilt, which we hope in time will become an heirloom too. Early log cabin quilts were sometimes called log house quilts, so we have called our quilt In the Log House. We wanted our heirloom quilt to be as near as possible to our antique quilt and found that the jelly roll Lilac Hill by Brannock & Patek was as close as we could get. We incorporated extra black fabric into the blocks and used black for the border to deepen the colouring.

There are thirty-six log cabin blocks in our quilt, rather more manageable than the 224 blocks in the antique quilt, so our quilt ended up measuring 66in x 66in (168cm x 168cm), which was great for throwing on a single bed. However, if you did want a larger quilt using two jelly rolls would allow you to make eighty log cabin blocks, which could be set in an 8 x 10 block layout and would measure 66in x 83in. Additional or wider borders could increase the size even more if required.

In the Log House Quilt

Vital Statistics

Finished Size:	66in x 66in
Block Size:	8¼in square
Number of Blocks:	36
Setting:	6 blocks x 6 blocks plus 2in first border, 1in second border and 5in third border

Requirements

- One jelly roll **OR** forty 2½in wide strips cut across the width of the fabric
- 2¼yd (2m) of black fabric for first and third border and additional fabric in the quilt
- 10in (25cm) of fabric for the second border
- ½yd (50cm) of binding fabric

SORTING THE STRIPS

- Divide the jelly roll into the following strips (two will be spare):
  - Eighteen dark strips.
  - Twenty light strips.

Cutting Tips

- When cutting the jelly roll strips in half along the length don't cut through more than one jelly roll strip at a time.
- Use a second ruler to check that you are not making your left-hand strip too wide – it is easy to do.
- Remember that if your left-hand strip is cut too wide then your right-hand strip is too narrow, doubling your inaccuracy.
- When cutting your rectangles you can layer your strips up to a maximum of four before losing accuracy. Press first to hold the layers together. You can butt your layers of strips next to each other to speed up cutting.

CUTTING INSTRUCTIONS

JELLY ROLL STRIPS:

- Dark strips: Cut each of the eighteen dark strips in half lengthways to create thirty-six strips 1¼in x 42in.
- From each of the thirty-six dark strips cut the following rectangles, *keeping the different sizes in separate piles*. Don't put the fabrics in any order as they need to be mixed up.
  - 1¼in x 2in.
  - 1¼in x 2¾in.
  - 1¼in x 4¼in.
  - 1¼in x 5in.
  - 1¼in x 5¾in.
  - 1¼in x 6½in.
  - 1¼in x 7¼in.
  - 1¼in x 8in.
- Light strips: cut each of the twenty light strips in half lengthways to create forty strips 1¼in x 42in.
- Take thirty-six of the strips and cut each into the following rectangles, *keeping the different sizes in separate piles*. Don't put the fabrics in any order as they need to be mixed up.
  - 1¼in x 1¼in.
  - 1¼in x 2in.
  - 1¼in x 2¾in.
  - 1¼in x 3½in.
  - 1¼in x 5in.
  - 1¼in x 5¾in.
  - 1¼in x 6½in.
  - 1¼in x 7¼in.
  - 1¼in x 8in.
- Cut each of the remaining four light 1¼in x 42in strips into nine rectangles 1¼in x 4¼in. You need thirty-six.

BLACK FABRIC:

- Cut six 2½in wide strips across the fabric width for the first border.
- Cut six 5½in wide strips across the fabric width for the third border.
- Cut fourteen 1¼in wide strips across the fabric width and subcut as follows:
  - Take nine and subcut each into four rectangles each 1¼in x 8¾in. You need thirty-six.
  - Take three and subcut each into twelve rectangles each 1¼in x 3½in. You need thirty-six.
  - Take two and subcut into thirty-six 1¼in x 1¼in squares.

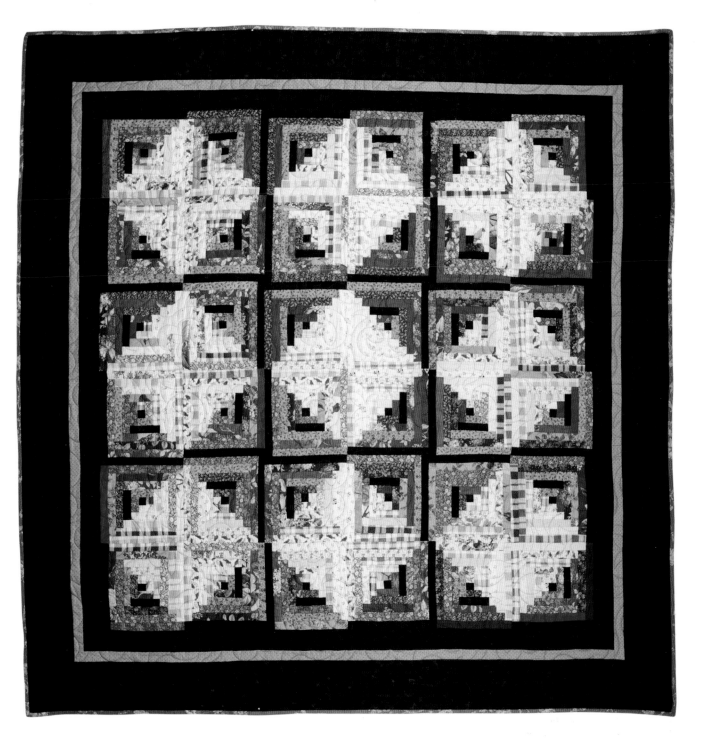

SECOND BORDER:

- Cut six 1½in wide strips across the width of the fabric.

BINDING:

- Cut seven 2½in wide strips across the width of the fabric.

CHECKLIST

You should have thirty-six each of these 1¼in wide light and dark strips (logs), as shown in the diagrams below.

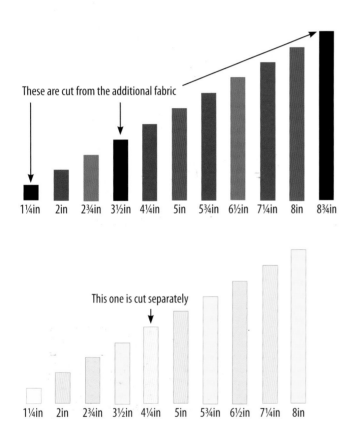

These are cut from the additional fabric

1¼in 2in 2¾in 3½in 4¼in 5in 5¾in 6½in 7¼in 8in 8¾in

This one is cut separately

1¼in 2in 2¾in 3½in 4¼in 5in 5¾in 6½in 7¼in 8in

SEWING THE LOG CABIN BLOCKS

When you are adding the strips or 'logs' to each block you can have them as scrappy as you like. Your black strips however will appear in the same place in every block and so will the light 4¼in strip that was cut from the same fabric.

1 Take a light 1¼in square and a black 1¼in centre square and with right sides together, sew together. Press away from the centre.

2 Sew a light 1¼in x 2in log to this unit. Press towards the outer log.

3 Sew on a dark 1¼in x 2in log as shown and press towards the outer log.

4 Now sew on a dark 1¼in x 2¾in log and press towards the outer log.

5 Sew on a light 1¼in x 2¾in log and press towards the outer log.

Sew on a light 1¼in x 3½in log and press towards the outer log.

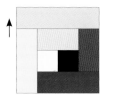

7 Sew on a black 1¼in x 3½in log and press towards the outer log.

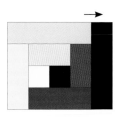

8 Sew on a dark 1¼in x 4¼in log and press towards the outer log.

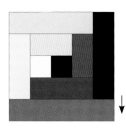

9 Continue sewing the light and dark logs in this manner until your first log cabin block is complete. Repeat steps 1–8 to make thirty-six blocks in total. Once you are familiar with the technique, chain piecing will speed the process. You can chain piece lots of step 1 before snipping them apart and pressing. You then chain piece step 2 to these units before snipping them apart and pressing, and so on.

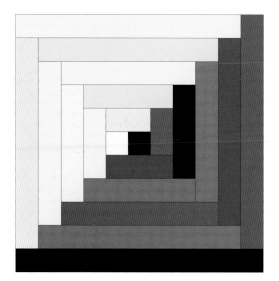

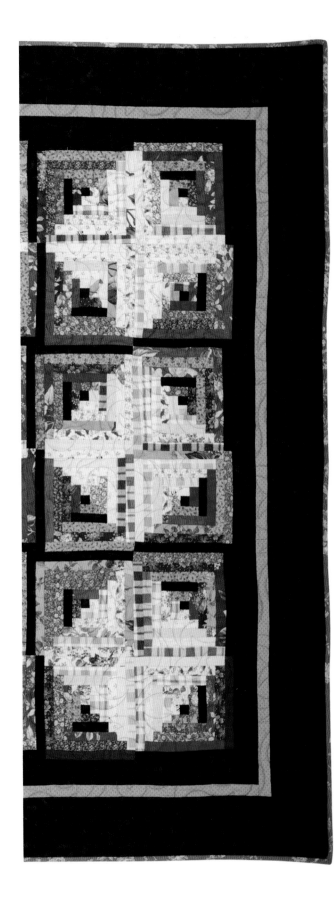

ASSEMBLING THE QUILT

10 Referring to the block diagram shown below lay out your blocks and when you are happy with the layout sew the blocks into rows and then sew the rows together, pinning at every seam intersection to ensure a perfect match.

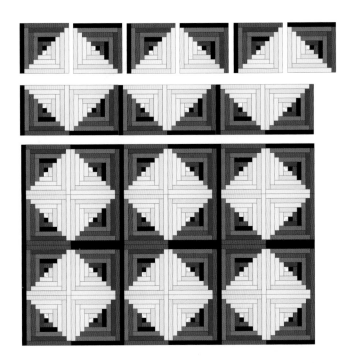

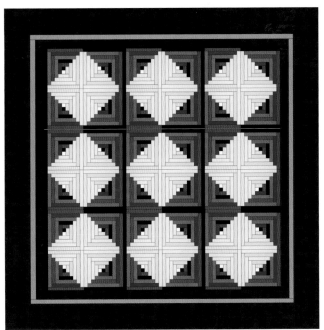

ADDING THE BORDERS

11 Join the first border strips into a continuous length. Determine the vertical measurement from top to bottom through the centre of your quilt top and cut two side borders to this measurement. Pin and sew to the quilt and press.

12 Now determine the horizontal measurement from side to side across the centre of the quilt top and cut two borders to this measurement. Sew to the top and bottom of your quilt and press. Repeat this process to add the second and third borders.

13 Your quilt top is now complete. Prepare the top, wadding (batting) and backing fabric for quilting and then quilt as desired – see advice in Quilting in General Techniques. Bind the quilt to finish, following the instructions in Binding a Quilt.

Heirloom Quilt Ideas

Log Cabin blocks can be arranged in many ways to create different patterns. Instead of using the arrangement we have chosen try a pattern called Starry Night, shown in the first diagram below. This Starry Night pattern could be adapted so the quilt is still using thirty-six blocks, as shown in the 6 x 6 layout.

NORTH COUNTRY WAYS

Antique Inspiration

This strip quilt is the palest mauve and lemon with a wool wadding (batting) and is beautifully hand quilted, as you would expect from a quilt from the North East of England. These quilts were often referred to as Durham quilts, however, quilts from this part of Britain were not all made in Durham. During the1920s when work was hard to find the Rural Industries Board decided that if they could not find work for the men they would find some work for the women and they chose quilting. All the women selected for the scheme not only had to be good quilters but also had to be means tested to be allowed on the scheme.

Only a few London retailers were authorized to sell the quilted products and Claridges Hotel in London gave them a large order for silk quilts. Subsequently, a headline appeared in the London papers reading, 'Durham Quilts for Claridges' and since then all quilts from the North East of England have been referred to as Durham quilts even though technically they were not all from Durham. This very successful scheme ended with the outbreak of the Second World War. The quilt measures 73in x 100in (185cm x 254cm).

Today's Heirloom

We were determined to have a Welsh or North Country strip quilt in this book as we have a great collection of these lovely quilts. Some careful thought and a little artistic licence were required for the design of our modern heirloom and in the end we used our jelly roll to piece alternate strips. We chose a jelly roll called Lately from London by Barbara Brackman, which not only had the right colours but also had the right name!

The layout looks complicated but in fact it is very easy as the strip-pieced units are cut into segments and rearranged into a Seminole pattern. Plain sashing and borders contrast nicely with the pieced sections and also give the opportunity for some lovely quilting. We used a longarm machine for our quilting but you could create your own machine or hand quilting patterns. The quilt was made by the authors and longarm quilted by The Quilt Room.

North Country Ways Quilt

Vital Statistics

Finished Size:	86in x 77in
Block Size/Setting:	8½in wide pieced vertical rows and 8in plain vertical rows
Number of Rows:	4 pieced and 5 plain vertical rows

Requirements

- One jelly roll **OR** forty 2½in wide strips cut across the width of the fabric
- 4yd (3.6m) of background fabric
- ¾yd (65cm) of binding fabric

SORTING YOUR FABRICS

- Choose eight of the lightest strips to be the centre of your strip units.
- Choose sixteen of the darkest strips to be the outer strips.
- The remaining sixteen will be classified as medium.

CUTTING INSTRUCTIONS

BACKGROUND FABRIC:

- Cut sixteen 3in wide strips across the width of the fabric.
- *Re-fold the fabric lengthways* and cut five 8½in wide strips down the length of the fabric. Set these aside for the plain vertical rows and they will be trimmed to size later (approximately 86in).

BINDING FABRIC:

- Cut nine 2½in wide strips across the width of the fabric.

SEWING THE STRIP UNITS

1 Select one light, two medium and two dark jelly roll strips and two 3in background strips and sew them together lengthways as shown in the diagram. Press the seams in one direction. Repeat to make eight strip units in total.

Make 8

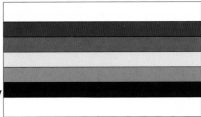

Background strip 3in wide
Dark jelly roll strip
Medium jelly roll strip
Light jelly roll strip
Medium jelly roll strip
Dark jelly roll strip
Background strip 3in wide

2 Cut each strip unit into sixteen 2½in segments to make a total of 128 segments. Eight segments are spare.

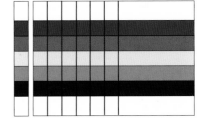

3 Select thirty segments randomly and sew together, off-setting them by one square as shown in the diagram. Pin at every seam intersection to ensure a perfect match. If you find the seams don't nest together nicely then rotate the segment so they do.

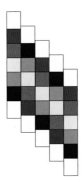

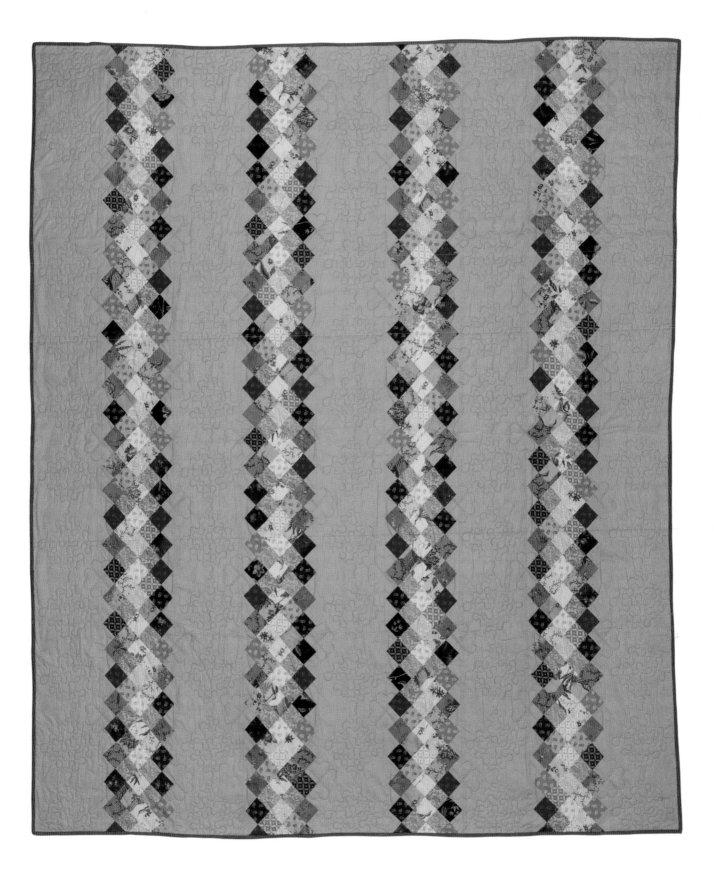

4 When you have sewn thirty segments together gently press the unit. Repeat to make four rows of thirty segments.

5 Take one row and cut the row into two pieces, cutting through the centre of a central square – your two pieces don't have to be the same length.

6 Swap the two pieces around so their straight edges are at the ends and then re-sew the row, joining the diagonal ends. Pin at every seam intersection to ensure a perfect match and then press.

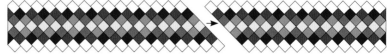

7 Using your longest quilting ruler, trim ½in away from the diamond points to straighten both the top and bottom edges. Repeat with all four rows.

ASSEMBLING THE QUILT

8 Measure the length of your pieced vertical rows and then trim the five 8½in background border strips to this measurement. It is important that they are all cut the same length.

9 When attaching the border strips to a vertical row, pin the centre and the ends of both the border strip and the vertical row together. You can then pin the rest, easing the strips if necessary.

10 Sew the five border strips and the four vertical rows together as shown in the diagram far right. Press the quilt top.

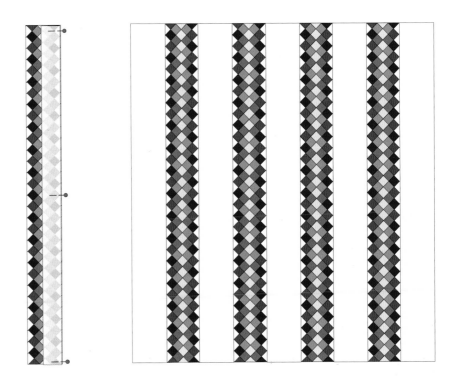

FINISHING THE QUILT

11 The quilt top is now complete. Prepare the top, wadding (batting) and backing fabric for quilting and quilt as desired – see Quilting in General Techniques. Bind the quilt to finish, following the instructions in Binding a Quilt.

BACK TO SCHOOL

Antique Inspiration

This mellow-coloured quilt is an American creation, featuring the very popular schoolhouse design, which was much admired during the second half of the 19th century. The design is thought to have originated in New Jersey, USA. Quilt blocks representing well-known objects in pictorial form, such as houses, boats, baskets, flowers and trees, have long been popular in patchwork and this charming quilt is a good example. The quilt has a calico backing with a thick cotton wadding (batting) and is machine pieced and hand quilted. It uses some very unusual fabrics, including one fabric with a fishing line, fishing hooks and fish, and although the fabrics look similar to those used in the 1920s they could be as late as the 1940s.

On a personal note, this quilt was one of a pair Pam bought on a trip to the USA with her friend and business partner, Rosemary Miller. When Rosemary retired they shared the collection and both Pam and Rosemary each now own one of the pair, which is rather a nice thought. The quilt measures 70in x 88in (178cm x 224cm).

Today's Heirloom

Inspired by the antique quilt's schoolhouse block and mellow colouring we chose fabrics from the delicate Mrs March Collection from Lecien for our heirloom quilt, which had the subtle colours we were looking for, together with a few bolder reds and greys. There are many house and schoolhouse blocks available today but we liked the fact that our schoolhouses are a little naïve as we feel that this design adds to the charm of the quilt. The block is easily created in three horizontal sections pieced together and the blocks are separated by very pale vertical and horizontal sashing.

We chose a dark backing fabric for the quilt to act as a contrast to the front and a grey binding to complete it and just loved the finished effect. The quilt was made by the authors and longarm quilted by The Quilt Room.

Back to School Quilt

Vital Statistics

Finished Size: 58in x 82in
Block Size: 12in x 14in
Number of Blocks: 20
Setting: 4 x 5 blocks plus 2in sashing and borders

Requirements

- One jelly roll **OR** forty 2½in wide strips cut across the width of the fabric
- 3¼yd (3m) of background fabric
- 20in (50cm) of binding fabric
- 60-degree triangle ruler

SORTING YOUR STRIPS

- Pair up the strips into strips of similar colours calling one of each pair Strip A and the other Strip B. The twenty Strip As will be used for the base of the schoolhouse and the twenty Strip Bs will be used for the roofs and chimneys.

CUTTING INSTRUCTIONS

JELLY ROLL STRIPS:

- Cut each Strip A as follows:
  - One 2½in x 6½in rectangle.
  - One 2½in x 7½in rectangle.
- Trim the blance of Strip A to measure 1½in wide and subcut as follows:
  - One 1½in x 6½in rectangle.
  - One 1½in x 7½in rectangle.
  - One 1½in x 12½in rectangle.
  (You might find it easier to cut all the rectangles 2½in wide and then trim to a width of 1½in – see which method you prefer.)
- Cut each Strip B as follows:
  - Two 2½in squares.
  - Two 2½in x 18in rectangles.

BACKGROUND FABRIC:

- Cut seven 1½in wide strips across the width of the fabric.
  - Subcut four strips into twenty 1½in x 7½in rectangles (five to each strip).
  - Subcut three strips into twenty 1½in x 6in rectangles (seven to each strip – one is spare).
- Cut three 4½in wide strips across the width of the fabric. Lay the 60-degree triangle ruler with the 5¼in line at the bottom of each strip and cut one triangle. The top of the triangle ruler will extend beyond the strip and you will find you have a flat top to your triangle which measures 1⅛in across.

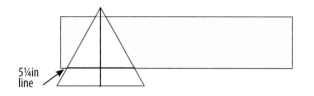

5¼in line

- Rotate the ruler 180 degrees and cut a second triangle. Continue along the strip and cut seven triangles from each of the three strips.

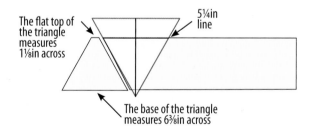

The flat top of the triangle measures 1⅛in across

5¼in line

The base of the triangle measures 6⅜in across

- Cut each triangle in half vertically to create forty end pieces for the roof sections.

- Open out the remaining fabric (approximately 86in) and fold *lengthways*. This is to avoid having joins in the sashing and borders. Trim the selvedge but not excessively as you need a width of 42½in to make your cuts.

- Cut seventeen 2½in strips lengthways.
  – Set two aside for the outer side border.
  – Take six and cut each into one 2½in x 56in rectangle and two 2½in x 14½in rectangles to make six 2½in x 56in rectangles for the vertical sashing and twelve 2½in x 14½in rectangles for the horizontal sashing.
  – Take one strip and cut three 2½in x 14½in rectangles and put these with the horizontal sashing just cut making fifteen in total.
  – Take two strips and cut twenty 2½in x 7½in rectangles.
  – Take three strips and cut each into thirteen 2½in x 6½in rectangles to make thirty-nine.
  – Take one strip and cut one 2½in x 6½in rectangle to add to the ones just cut to make a total of forty 2½in x 6½in rectangles. Then cut twenty 2½in x 3½in rectangles.
  – Take two strips and cut into forty 2½in x 3in rectangles. You will have approximately 50in excess, which is spare.

BINDING FABRIC:
- Cut seven 2½in wide strips across the width of the fabric.

CHECKLIST FOR EACH BLOCK
JELLY ROLL STRIP A:
- One 2½in x 6½in rectangle.
- One 2½in x 7½in rectangle.
- One 1½in x 6½in rectangle.
- One 1½in x 7½in rectangle.
- One 1½in x 12½in rectangle.

JELLY ROLL STRIP B:
- Two 2½in x 2½in squares.
- Two 2½in x 18in rectangles.

BACKGROUND:
- One 2½in x 7½in rectangle.
- Two 2½in x 6½in rectangles.
- One 2½in x 6in rectangle.
- Two 2½in x 3in rectangles.
- One 2½in x 3½in rectangle.

SEWING THE SCHOOLHOUSE

1 Sew two background 2½in x 6½in rectangles together with one 2½in x 6½in house rectangle and one 1½in x 6½in house rectangle as shown. Press seams in one direction.

2 Sew a 1½in x 7½in background rectangle to the top of this unit and press. This is the right side of the schoolhouse.

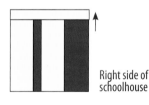

Right side of schoolhouse

3 Sew a 2½in x 7½in background rectangle between a 2½in x 7½in house rectangle and a 1½in x 7½in house rectangle as shown and press. This is the left side of the schoolhouse.

Left side of schoolhouse

4 Sew the right and the left sides of the schoolhouse together and press as shown.

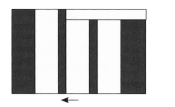

5 Sew a 1½in x 12½in house rectangle to the house base to complete Unit A and press as shown.

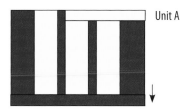

Unit A

SEWING THE ROOF SECTION

6 Sew the two Strip B 2½in x 18in rectangles together as shown and press.

7 Position the 60-degree triangle to the left of the strip with the 4½in line of the ruler on the bottom of the strip. Cut the roof triangle.

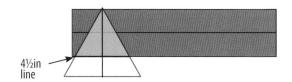

4½in line

8 Using your normal quilting ruler make another cut 5½in parallel to the cut of the roof triangle. The rest of the strip is spare: we did consider cutting this up to make our binding but decided in the end to set it aside for a future project.

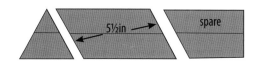

5½in   spare

9 Take a 1½in x 6in background rectangle and sew to the left side of the larger roof section. Press away from the background rectangle and using your ruler trim as shown. *Note*: before sewing, flip the rectangle back to make sure you have sufficient rectangle at each end to create a straight edge.

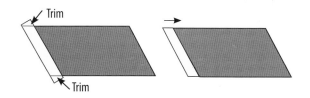

Trim

Trim

10 Sew the roof triangle to this unit and press away from the background fabric.

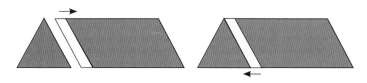

11 Sew a background roof end piece to both ends to complete Unit B and press seams away from the background fabric.

Unit B

12 Sew two 2½in Strip B squares together with one 3½in background rectangle in the centre and two 2½in x 3in background rectangles at each end.

13 Press the seams away from the background rectangles. This is Unit C.

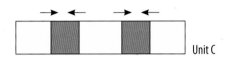

Unit C

14 Sew Units A, B and C together to make the block. It should measure 12in x 14in. Press the seams as shown.

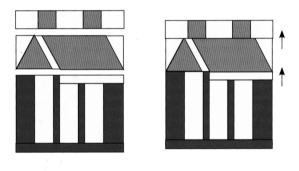

ADDING THE SASHING AND BORDER STRIPS

15 Lay out your blocks and when you are happy with the layout, sew the four schoolhouse blocks in row one together with a 2½in x 14½in sashing strip in between. Press away from the sashing strips. Repeat to make five rows in total.

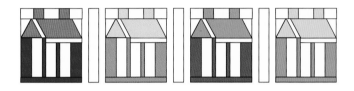

16 Measure the width of the rows and trim all six horizontal sashing strips to the same length. It is important they are all trimmed to the same length in order to keep the quilt square.

18 Measure the length of the quilt and trim the two side borders to this measurement. Pin and sew these borders to the quilt.

17 Pin and sew a horizontal sashing strip to the top and bottom of the first row and to the bottom of the other five rows. When joining the sashing to a row, mark the centre of both the sashing strip and the row and pin in position. Then pin at both ends and continue pinning in position, easing if necessary. Sew the rows together. Press away from the sashing strips.

FINISHING THE QUILT

19 The quilt top is now complete. Prepare the top, wadding (batting) and backing fabric for quilting and quilt as desired – see Quilting in General Techniques. Bind the quilt to finish, following the instructions in Binding a Quilt.

CELEBRATION TIME

Antique Inspiration

This interesting antique quilt is from the North East of England and has a framed patchwork design on one side and a chintz fabric on the other, with a wool wadding (batting) in between them. The fabrics used on the patchwork design denote a quilt from about 1880, although the quilt might be earlier.

The quilt is a medallion type where a central design, in this case a star block, forms the focal point of the quilt, with borders or 'frames' building out from the central area. The quilting patterns used in the quilt include classic northern favourites such as lined twist, braid and a simple bellows. The interesting fact is that it has been quilted from the chintz side in a strippy design, which possibly means that the chintz was intended as the top or 'best' side and that the pieced side is the everyday or working side. The quilt measures 78in x 84in (198cm x 213cm).

Today's Heirloom

As nice as the chintz side of the antique quilt is, our interest is in the patchwork side and its framed design starting from the centre and working outwards. For our modern-day heirloom quilt we have used a little artistic licence to make it jelly roll friendly and have chosen to use the bright sunny colours from Tanya Whelan's Delilah collection, mixed with a soft white. The jelly roll provides the array of colours all packaged up for us and the addition of 4⅛ yards (3.75 metres) of background fabric provided us with a good bed-sized quilt. Our outer border fabric from the Delilah range sets off the quilt beautifully.

This quilt is great fun and rewarding to make and has nine borders in total, including a sawtooth design, flying geese and a four-patch border. The name of the quilt comes from the fact that The Quilt Room used this quilt as a Celebration Block of the Month to celebrate its 30th anniversary. We don't think we could have chosen a more beautiful quilt. It was made by the authors and longarm quilted by The Quilt Room.

Celebration Time Quilt

Vital Statistics

Finished Size: 84in x 84in

Setting: Medallion – 16in central block surrounded by nine borders of varying widths

Requirements

- One jelly roll **OR** forty 2½in wide strips cut across the width of the fabric
- 4⅛yd (3.75m) of background fabric
- 1⅛yd (1m) of outer border fabric
- 24in (60cm) of binding fabric
- Multi-Size 45/90 or similar ruler for cutting half-square triangles from strips

SORTING YOUR STRIPS

- Choose four for the centre stars, either in similar colours or different. The diagram below identifies the quilt layout.
- Choose two strips for Border 1 in similar colours.
- Choose six mixed strips for piano keys Border 2.
- Choose three similar colours for the sawtooth Border 3.
- Choose ten similar colours for the flying geese Border 5.
- Choose fifteen assorted strips for the four-patch Border 7.

CUTTING INSTRUCTIONS

JELLY ROLL STRIPS:

- Cut each of the four strips allocated for the centre stars into sixteen 2½in squares. You will need twelve squares from each strip for the centre stars, four squares for the corners of Border 1 and four squares for the corners of Border 4. Eight will be spare.
- Cut each of the two strips allocated for Border 1 into two rectangles 2½in x 16½in to make four in total.
- Leave the six strips allocated for the piano keys Border 2 uncut.
- Cut each of the three strips allocated for the sawtooth Border 3 in half to make six half strips 2½in x 21in approximately.
- Cut each of the ten strips allocated for the flying geese Border 5 into eight rectangles 2½in x 4½in. You need 80 in total.
- Cut each of the fifteen strips allocated for the four-patch Border 7 in half to make thirty half strips 2½in x 21in approximately.

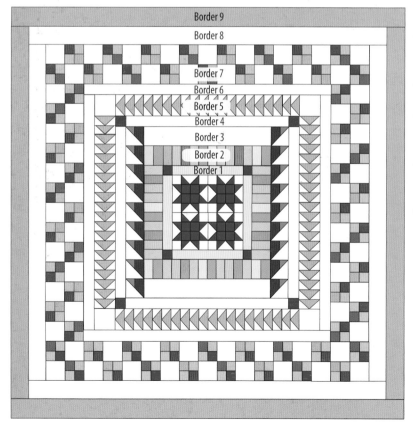

BACKGROUND FABRIC:

- Cut nineteen 4½in wide strips across the width of the fabric.
  - Subcut eight into sixty 4½in squares for Border 7.
  - Cut two in half to create four half strips approximately 4½in x 21in. Three half strips are for sawtooth Border 3 and cut the remaining half strip into four 4½in squares for the corners of flying geese Border 5.
  - Leave nine strips uncut for Border 3 and Border 8.
- Cut twenty-two 2½in wide strips across the fabric width.
  - Subcut eleven into 2½in squares to make a total of 176. Sixteen of these are for the star centre and 160 are for the flying geese Border 5.
  - Cut two into eight 2½in x 4½in rectangles to make sixteen for the star centre.
  - Leave nine uncut, four for Border 4 and five for Border 6.

OUTER BORDER FABRIC:

- Cut eight 4½in wide strips across the width of the fabric.

BINDING FABRIC:

- Cut eight 2½in wide strips across the width of the fabric.

MAKING THE CENTRE STAR BLOCK

1 You can either make four stars in different fabrics or make them scrappy as we have done. Take one 2½in square allocated for the centre stars and lay it right sides together on a 2½in x 4½in background rectangle. Sew across the diagonal. If it helps, draw the diagonal line first or make a fold to mark your stitching line.

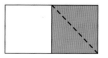

2 Flip the square over and press as shown. Trim the excess jelly roll fabric but do not trim the background fabric. Although this creates a little more bulk it helps to keep your work in shape.

3 Sew another 2½in square allocated for the centre stars to the other side of the background rectangle. Press and trim the excess background fabric.

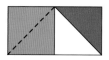

4 Repeat the process in steps 1–3 to make a total of sixteen flying geese units.

Make 16

5 Sew a 2½in background square to both sides of a flying geese unit and press towards the background squares. Repeat to make eight units.

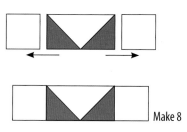

Make 8

6 Sew four 2½in jelly roll squares together to form the centre of a star. Sew a flying geese unit to both sides as shown. Press towards the centre. Repeat to make four of these units.

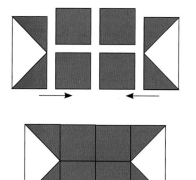

Make 4

7 Join the units together, pinning at every seam intersection to ensure a perfect match. Repeat to make four stars. Press two stars with the seams as shown on the left-hand diagram and two stars with the seams pressed as shown on the right-hand diagram.

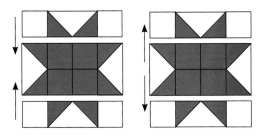

8 Sew four stars together to form the centre of the medallion quilt, pinning at every seam intersection to ensure a perfect match. *Note*: there will be occasions when a seam needs to be re-pressed in a different direction.

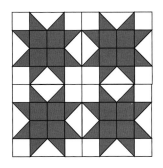

MAKING BORDER 1

9 Sew two strips allocated for Border 1 to the sides of the centre star and press as shown. Sew two 2½in squares allocated for the corner squares to both sides of the other two 2½in x 16½in strips and press as shown. Sew the units together, pinning at the seam intersections to ensure a perfect match.

MAKING BORDER 2

10 Sew four of the strips allocated for the piano keys border together lengthways and press seams in one direction. Subcut into eight 4½in segments.

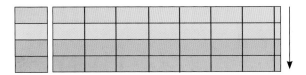

11 Sew two of the strips allocated for the piano keys border together lengthways and press as shown. Subcut into eight 4½in segments.

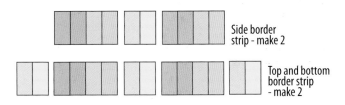

12 Sew the side border strips together as shown and then sew the top and bottom border strips together as shown.

Side border strip - make 2

Top and bottom border strip - make 2

13 Pin and sew to the quilt top, easing if necessary. Your quilt top should now measure 28½in square.

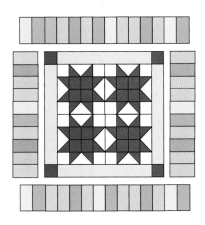

MAKING SAWTOOTH BORDER 3

14 Pair up the six half strips allocated for the sawtooth border, so you have two different fabrics in each pair. With right sides together, sew each pair down the long side to make three strip units. Open and press.

15 With right sides together, lay this unit on a 4½in background half strip aligning the edges and press to hold in place. Trim the left-hand selvedge. Position the Multi-Size 45/90 ruler, lining up the 4in mark at the bottom edge of the strips and cut the first triangle. You will notice that the cut out triangle has a flat top. This would just have been a dog ear you needed to cut off so it is saving you time.

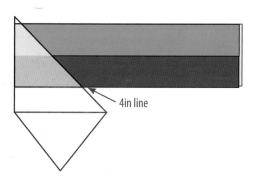

4in line

16 Rotate the ruler 180 degrees and cut the next triangle. Repeat to cut six pairs of triangles from the strip unit.

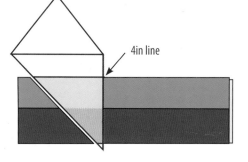

4in line

17 On each pair of triangles sew along the diagonals. Trim all dog ears and press open to form six half-square triangle units. Repeat with the other strip units to make a total of eighteen half-square triangle units.

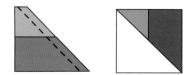

Make 18

18 Sew nine units together as shown for the left-hand border and nine together for the right-hand border.

Border 3
left side

Border 3
right side

19 Take two uncut 4½in background strips and trim both to measure 4½in x 28½in. Sew to the top and bottom of the quilt top and then press.

20 Sew on the sawtooth borders to the left and right sides of the quilt top as shown, easing if necessary. Your quilt top should now measure 36½in square.

MAKING BORDER 4

21 Take four uncut 2½in background strips and trim them to 2½in x 36½in. Sew them to the sides of the quilt top. Sew a 2½in corner square to both ends of the other two strips and sew to the top and bottom of the quilt top. Your quilt top should now measure 40½in square.

MAKING FLYING GEESE BORDER 5

22 Using the technique described for making flying geese units under Making the Centre Star Block steps 1–5, take the eighty 2½in x 4½in rectangles allocated for the flying geese border and sew a 2½in background square to both ends. Make eighty flying geese units.

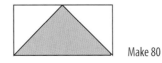

Make 80

23 Sew twenty flying geese units together to make one border and press. Repeat to make four borders.

24 Sew two borders to the sides of the quilt top as shown, easing where necessary. Press the seams. Sew a 4½in background square to both sides of the remaining two borders and sew to the top and bottom of the quilt top, easing if necessary. Press the seams. Your quilt top should now measure 48½in square.

MAKING BORDER 6
25 Sew five 2½in background strips into a continuous length and press. Cut two lengths 2½in x 48½in and two lengths 2½in x 52½in. Sew to the quilt top, easing if necessary. Your quilt top should now measure 52½in square.

MAKING FOUR-PATCH BORDER 7

26 Take two half strips allocated for the four-patch border and with right sides together sew down the long side. Open and press towards the darker side. Cut eight 2½in segments from this strip unit.

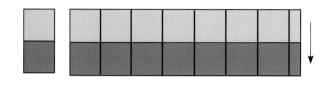

27 Repeat with all thirty half strips to make a total of 120 2½in segments. For speed you can layer one strip unit right sides together with another, reversing light and dark. The seams will nest together nicely. When you subcut your 2½in wide segments, they will be ready to sew together to make your four-patch blocks.

28 Chain piece the 2½in wide segments together to form sixty four-patch blocks. Cut the threads and press the four-patch blocks open.

Make 60

29 With right sides together, sew a 4½in background square to one side of a four-patch block. Repeat to make sixty units.

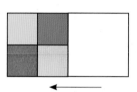

30 Sew thirteen of these units together as shown, pinning at every seam intersection. Make two side borders like this.

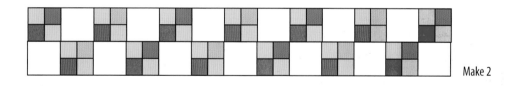

Make 2

31 Sew seventeen of the units together as shown, pinning at every seam intersection. Make a top and bottom border like this.

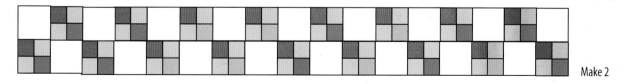

Make 2

32 Pin and sew the side borders on first and press. Pin and sew the top and bottom borders and press. Your quilt top should now measure 68½in square.

MAKING BORDER 8

33 Join the seven 4½in uncut border strips into a continuous length. Determine the vertical measurement from top to bottom through the centre of your quilt top, which should measure 68½in at this stage. Cut two side borders to this measurement. Pin and sew to the quilt and press. Now determine the horizontal measurement from side to side across the centre of the quilt top. Cut two borders to this measurement. Sew to the top and bottom of your quilt and press.

MAKING BORDER 9

34 Join the eight outer border strips into a continuous length. Cut and sew to the quilt top as described for Border 8.

FINISHING THE QUILT

35 The quilt top is now complete. Prepare the top, wadding (batting) and backing fabric for quilting and quilt as desired – see Quilting in General Techniques. Bind the quilt to finish, following the instructions in Binding a Quilt.

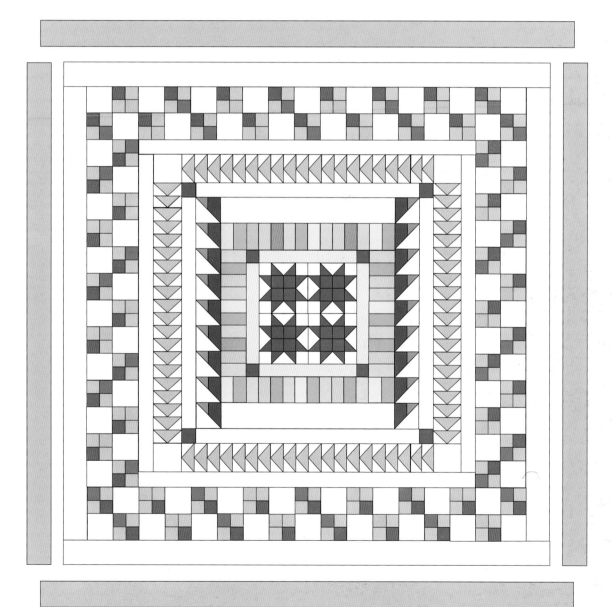

OCEAN WAVES

Antique Inspiration

This American quilt dates from the late 1930s and has a lovely mix of fabrics including some interesting orange and green. This design would have been perfect as a scrap quilt, allowing the maker to use up precious scraps of fabrics and old clothing and household textiles during the Great Depression era. Quilts such as these can also be used by the quilter to recall the history of a family, as the pieces used can come from many sources such as wedding clothes, baby's blankets and children's garments.

The Ocean Waves block is a traditional one dating back to the early 1900s and was one of many blocks that used triangles in inventive ways. The triangles can be arranged to create movement depending on which direction they point in and how the blocks are turned. This antique quilt was bought as a quilt top and was wadded and backed and then longarm quilted by the Quilt Room. The quilt measures 90in x 90in (229cm x 229cm).

Today's Heirloom

In keeping with the name of this traditional design, we chose to use a lovely blue jelly roll together with a white-on-white background fabric, which creates a wonderfully bright and fresh looking quilt. The design looks complex but it is really just a repeat of one simple block – however we can't deny that there are quite a few half-square triangles to make! If you like red and white quilts too then using a red-based jelly roll would be another option.

The Ocean Wave block is also known as Hovering Hawk and Road to Heaven and when it is set in rows with alternate blocks rotated by 90 degrees it creates a secondary pattern of plain squares, which could be emphasized further by hand or machine motif quilting. This quilt was made by Sharon Chambers from The Quilt Room and longarm quilted by The Quilt Room.

Ocean Waves Quilt

Vital Statistics

Finished Size:	64in x 80in
Block Size:	8in square
Number of Blocks:	80
Setting:	8 x 10 blocks

Requirements

- One jelly roll **OR** forty 2½in strips cut across the width of the fabric
- 4⅜yd (4m) of background fabric
- 24in (60cm) of binding fabric
- Multi-Size 45/90 ruler for cutting half-square triangles from strips

SORTING YOUR STRIPS

- Allocate thirty-two strips for the half-square triangle units.
- Allocate seven strips for the extra triangles.
- One strip is spare.

CUTTING INSTRUCTIONS

BACKGROUND FABRIC:

- Cut thirty-nine 2½in wide strips across the width of the fabric.
    - Thirty-two are needed for the half-square triangle units and seven are needed for the extra triangles.
- Cut ten 4⅞in strips across the width of the fabric.
    - Subcut each 4⅞in strip into eight 4⅞in squares to make a total of eighty squares.
    - Cut each square in half diagonally to make a total of 160 triangles.

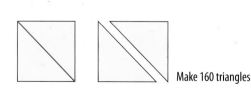

Make 160 triangles

BINDING FABRIC:

- Cut eight 2½in wide strips across the width of the fabric.

MAKING THE HALF-SQUARE TRIANGLE UNITS

1 Take a jelly roll strip and a 2½in background strip and press right sides together ensuring that they are *exactly* one on top of the other. The pressing will help hold the two strips together.

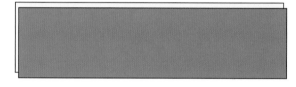

2 Lay them out on a cutting mat and position the Multi-Size 45/90 ruler as shown in the diagram, lining up the 2in mark at the bottom edge of the strips. Trim the selvedge and cut the first triangle. You will notice that the cut out triangle has a flat top. This would just have been a dog ear you needed to cut off so it is saving you time.

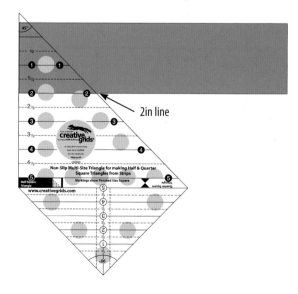

2in line

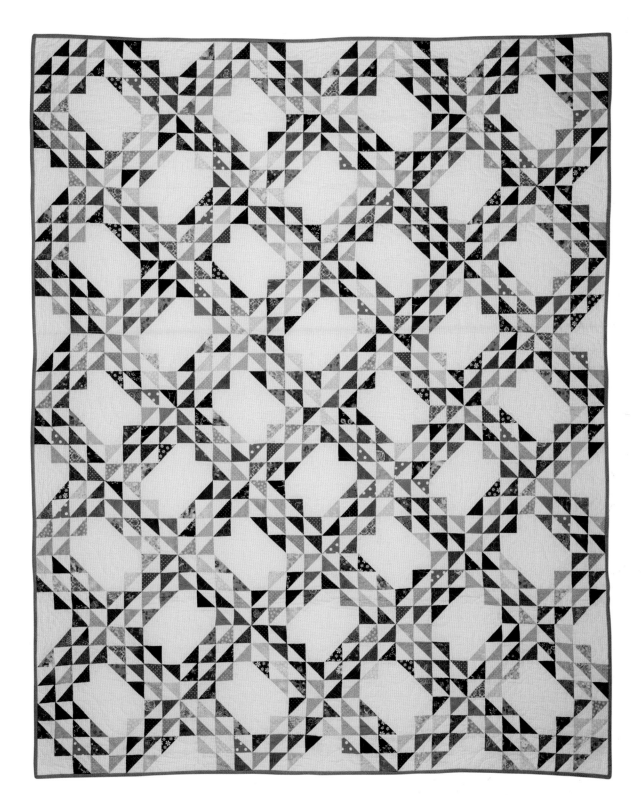

3 Rotate the ruler 180 degrees as shown in the diagram below and then cut the next triangle. Continue along the strip cutting the required amount of triangles. Cut twenty-five triangles from each strip.

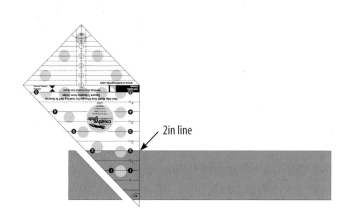

2in line

4 Sew along the diagonal of each pair of triangles. Trim the dog ears and press open towards the jelly roll fabric to form twenty-five half-square triangle units. Repeat with all thirty-two jelly roll strips allocated for the half-square triangle units. You need 800 half-square triangle units in total.

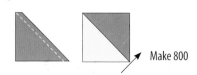

Make 800

5 Take the seven jelly roll strips allocated for the extra triangles and using the Multi-Size 45/90 cut each strip into twenty-five triangles. You can layer three or four strips together to speed up the cutting process but do not layer too many as you will lose accuracy. You need 160 extra jelly roll triangles in total.

Make 160

6 Repeat this with the seven background strips allocated for the extra triangles. You need 160 extra background triangles in total.

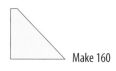

Make 160

ASSEMBLING THE BLOCKS

7 Take four half-square triangle units and sew together, pinning at every seam intersection to ensure a perfect match. Press as shown in the diagram. Repeat to make 160 of Unit A.

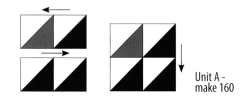

Unit A - make 160

8 Take one half-square triangle unit and sew one extra jelly roll triangle to each side as shown. Sew this unit to a large background triangle. Repeat to make 80 of Unit B.

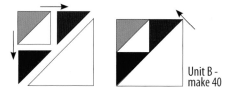

Unit B - make 40

9 Take one half-square triangle unit and sew one extra background triangle to each side as shown. Sew this unit to a large background triangle. Repeat to make 80 of Unit C.

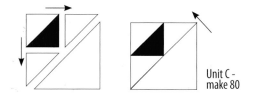

Unit C - make 80

10 Take two Unit As, one Unit B and one Unit C and sew together as shown, pinning at every seam intersection to ensure a perfect match. Repeat to make eighty blocks.

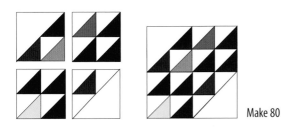

Make 80

Heirloom Quilt Ideas

You could experiment with the quilt layout in many ways. For example, you could add sashing between the blocks and make Unit Bs to create a secondary pattern as cornerposts.

You could also make other blocks to alternate with the Ocean blocks, such as the Barn Raising block shown here, which is also formed from half-square triangle units.

ASSEMBLING THE QUILT

11 Care must be taken now, so familiarize yourself with the block. Notice the position of the two dark triangles in one corner and the three dark triangles in the corner diagonally opposite.

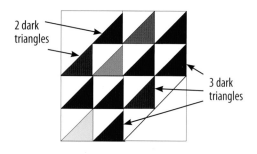

2 dark triangles

3 dark triangles

12 Take eight blocks and place them with the corners having the two dark triangles at *top left*. Now rotate alternate blocks 90 degrees to the *left*. Do not make the mistake of rotating them to the right – take care with this. Sew together to form row one, pinning at every seam intersection to ensure a perfect match. Press the seams to the right.

Move alternate blocks 90 degrees to the left

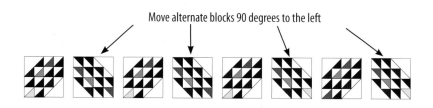

13 Make ten rows, taking care with the placement of the blocks and pressing all seams to the left. It is helpful to label the left-hand block to avoid any confusion later.

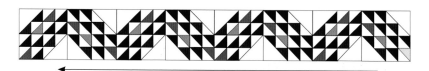

14 Lay out the ten rows ensuring the left-hand block is always on the left-hand side. Rotate the second, fourth, sixth and eighth rows 180 degrees.

15 Sew the rows together, pinning at every seam intersection to ensure a perfect match. Double check all the time to make sure you are positioning the blocks correctly. This is definitely a time for 'check twice, sew once'!

FINISHING THE QUILT

16 The quilt top is now complete. Prepare the top, wadding (batting) and backing fabric for quilting and quilt as desired – see Quilting in General Techniques. Bind the quilt to finish, following the instructions in Binding a Quilt.

TUMBLING BLOCKS

Antique Inspiration

This amazing quilt dates from just before the First World War and was made by Rosa Lee Gibson and her mother Etta Gibson between 1910 and 1915. It was left unfinished until Rosa's daughter Callie Gibson Clifton finished and quilted it seventy years later in 1985. This quilt therefore shows the patchwork and quilting skills of three generations of one family. This was the only one of our antique quilts that had a label. It is lovely to know this information about the makers and why adding a label to your quilt is always a good idea.

    This work of art contains a gorgeous array of sumptuous fabrics and the tiny diamonds that make up the tumbling blocks pattern have all been hand pieced. The three-dimensional appearance of this well-known block is created by the clever use of light, medium and dark tones. The quilt measures 64in x 84in (163cm x 214cm).

Today's Heirloom

It was a daunting task trying to replicate such a gorgeous quilt. It was also a challenge to create the design simply and with no set-in seams. We hope you agree that this is a quick and easy method that goes together beautifully. The three-dimensional effect of Tumbling Blocks is made by the correct mix of dark, medium and light fabrics. We found our darks and mediums in Panier de Fleurs from French General, which gave a good mix of dark blues and reds, plus it also had lots of greys that could be used as our medium fabrics. We added a cream-on-cream fabric as additional fabric, which became our light.

Piecing the quilt in vertical rows means you don't have any set-in seams and once you get started it really does go together quickly – or relatively quickly given the complexity of the pattern! The quilt was made by the authors and longarm quilted by the Quilt Room.

Tumbling Blocks Quilt

Vital Statistics

Finished Size: 60in x 64in
Setting: 26 vertical rows of 16 units each, plus 5in top and bottom border units and 4½in side borders

Requirements

- One jelly roll **OR** forty 2½in wide strips cut across the width of the fabric
- 3½yd (3.25m) of light fabric **OR** forty assorted light 3in wide strips cut across the fabric width
- 1¾yd (1.5m) of border fabric
- Jelly roll strips can be used for binding
- 60-degree triangle ruler

SORTING YOUR FABRICS

- Sort the jelly roll into sixteen dark strips and sixteen medium strips. The eight remaining can be used for the binding.

CUTTING INSTRUCTIONS

LIGHT FABRIC:
- Cut forty 3in wide strips across the width of the fabric.

BORDER FABRIC:
- Cut eleven 5in wide strips across the width of the fabric.
  - Set four aside for the side borders.
  - Keep the remaining seven strips folded and subcut each strip into eight 2½in x 5in rectangles. Still keeping the folded pairs together, lay a 60-degree triangle as far to the right as you can, as shown and with the 2½in line at the bottom cut a 60-degree edge. Your folded pairs of rectangles will give you twenty-six with the angle in one direction and twenty-six with the angle in the other direction. These are the end pieces for each vertical row. You will have four spare.

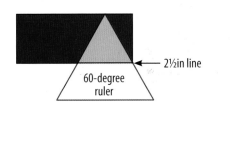

60-degree ruler — 2½in line

Make 26   Make 26

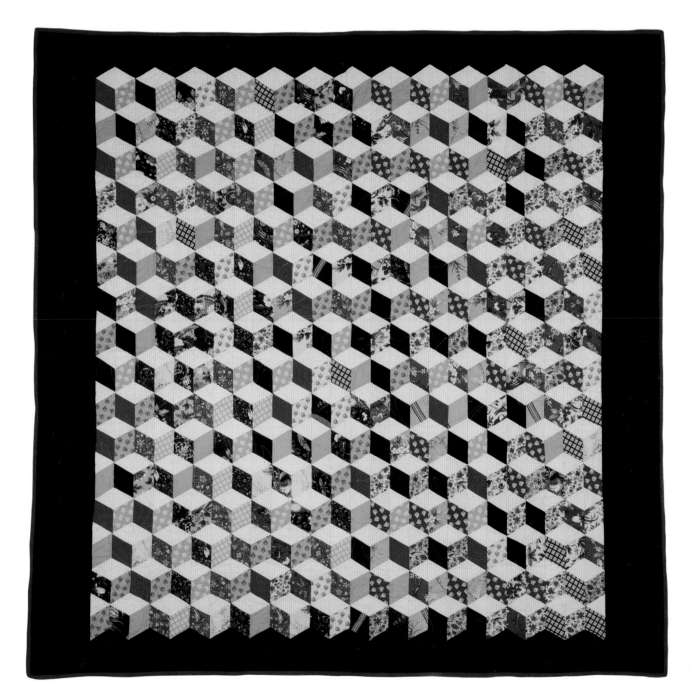

MAKING THE STRIP-PIECED UNITS

1 Sew a dark jelly roll strip to both sides of a 3in light strip to make Unit A. Press seams in one direction. Repeat to make sixteen Strip Unit As.

Strip Unit A
– make 16

2 Sew a medium jelly roll strip to both sides of a 3in light strip to make Unit B. Press seams in one direction. Repeat to make sixteen Strip Unit Bs.

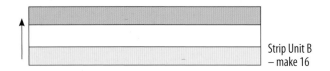

Strip Unit B
– make 16

3 Lay one Unit A on top of one Unit B with right sides together. Align the top and bottom edges and ensure the seams are pointing in opposite directions so they nest together nicely. It is important to always place Unit A on top of Unit B.

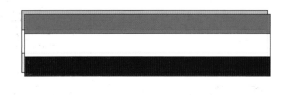

4 Lay a 60-degree triangle as far to the left of the strip units as possible and cut a 60-degree angled edge.

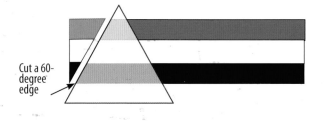

Cut a 60-degree edge

5 Using your quilting ruler cut thirteen 2½in wide segments across the width of the strip unit. Stop to check every few cuts that you are still cutting at a 60-degree angle.

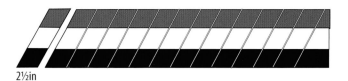

2½in

6 You now have thirteen segments from Strip Unit A and thirteen segments from Strip Unit B. Cut across each of the centre light diamonds, as shown.

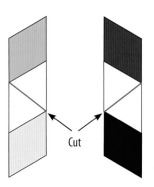

Cut

7 Keep the twenty-six medium units that will make the right-hand side of the tumbling block in one pile, and the twenty-six dark units that will make the left-hand side of the tumbling block in another pile.

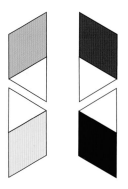

8 Repeat with all sixteen Strip Unit As and Strip Unit Bs to make a total of 416 dark units in one pile and 416 medium units in the other pile.

ASSEMBLING THE QUILT

9 The quilt is assembled by sewing the units into vertical rows and then sewing the vertical rows together. *Note*: if your quilt requires careful placement of colours you will need to lay all your blocks out before sewing the vertical rows together. Start Row 1 with a dark unit and sew it right sides together with a medium unit. When you sew the units together you will have an overlap at each end as shown in the diagram. Check as you sew that you are forming straight edges to your vertical rows. Sew sixteen units together and sew an end piece to both ends to complete one row. Press seams downwards.

10 Start Row 2 with a medium unit. Sew sixteen units together and sew an end piece to both ends to complete one row. Press seams upwards.

11 Sew Row 1 to Row 2, pinning at every seam intersection to ensure a perfect match. Press the seams.

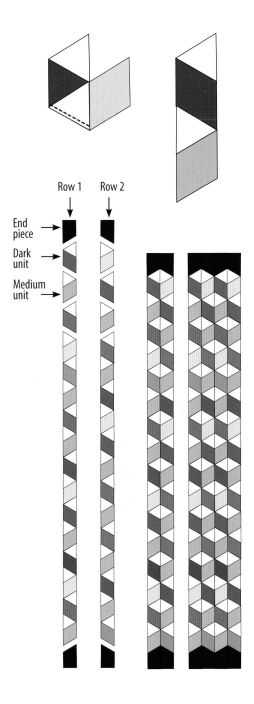

12 Repeat to sew thirteen pairs of Row 1 and Row 2, and then sew the pairs of vertical rows together.

ADDING THE SIDE BORDERS

13 Determine the vertical measurement from top to bottom through the centre of your quilt top. Join two border strips together to form one side border and two border strips together to form the other side border. Trim to the vertical measurement and pin and sew to both sides of the quilt top. Press the work.

FINISHING THE QUILT

14 The quilt top is now complete. Prepare the top, wadding (batting) and backing fabric for quilting and quilt as desired – see Quilting in General Techniques. Bind the quilt to finish, following the instructions in Binding a Quilt.

GENERAL TECHNIQUES

TOOLS

All the projects in this book require rotary cutting equipment. You will need a self-healing cutting mat at least 18in x 24in and a rotary cutter. We recommend the 45mm or the 60mm diameter rotary cutter. Any rotary cutting work requires rulers and most people have a make they prefer. We like the Creative Grids rulers as their markings are clear, they do not slip on fabric and their Turn-a-Round facility is so useful when dealing with half-inch measurements. We recommend the 6½in x 24in as a basic ruler plus a large square no less than 12½in, which is handy for squaring up and making sure you are always cutting at right angles.

We have tried not to use too many speciality rulers but when working with 2½in wide strips you do have to re-think some cutting procedures. You do need a speciality ruler to cut half-square triangles and quarter-square triangles, which you will find in some of our quilts. Creative Grids have designed the Multi-Size 45/90 ruler for us, which is perfect. Whichever ruler you decide to use, please make sure you are lining up your work on the correct markings.

The Multi-Size 45/90 shows the *finished* size measurements. This means that when you are cutting half-square triangles from 2½in strips you need to line up the 2in marking along the bottom of the strip. This 2in marking indicates that the finished half-square triangle unit will be 2in. If you are using a different ruler, please do make sure that you are lining up your work on the correct markings. The Easy Angle ruler for example shows the *unfinished* size and it will be the 2½in mark that will be lined up with the bottom of the strip.

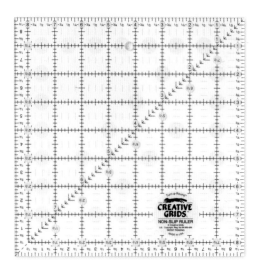

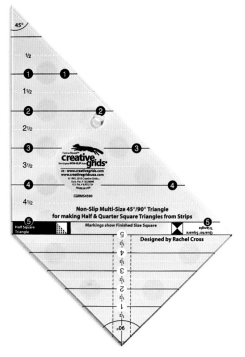

We quilters all have our favourite rulers. We like to use the Creative Grids rulers and squares, some of which are shown here, including the Multi-Size 45/90 for cutting half-square and quarter-square triangles.

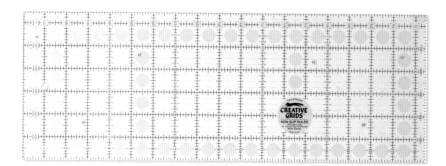

SEAMS

We cannot stress enough the importance of maintaining an accurate ¼in seam allowance throughout. We prefer to say an accurate *scant* ¼in seam because there are two factors to take into account. Firstly, the thickness of thread and secondly, when the seam allowance is pressed to one side it takes up a tiny amount of fabric. These are both extremely small amounts but if they are ignored you will find your *exact* ¼in seam allowance is taking up more than ¼in. So, it is well worth testing your seam allowance before starting on a quilt and most sewing machines have various needle positions that can be used to make any adjustments.

SEAM ALLOWANCE TEST

Take a 2½in strip and cut off three segments each 1½in wide. Sew two segments together down the longer side and press the seam to one side. Sew the third segment across the top. It should fit exactly. If it doesn't, you need to make an adjustment to your seam allowance. If it is too long, your seam allowance is too wide and can be corrected by moving the needle on your sewing machine to the right. If it is too small, your seam allowance is too narrow and this can be corrected by moving the needle to the left.

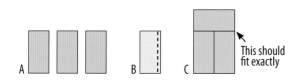

A   B   C   This should fit exactly

PRESSING

In quiltmaking, pressing is of vital importance and if extra care is taken you will be well rewarded. This is especially true when dealing with strips. If your strips start bowing and stretching you will lose accuracy.

- Always set your seam after sewing by pressing the seam as sewn, without opening up your strips. This eases any tension and prevents the seam line from distorting. Move the iron with an up and down motion, zigzagging along the seam rather than ironing down the length of the seam, which could cause distortion.

- Open up your strips and press on the *right* side of the fabric towards the darker fabric, if necessary guiding the seam underneath to make sure the seam is going in the right direction. Press with an up and down motion rather than along the length of the strip.

- Always take care if using steam and certainly don't use steam anywhere near a bias edge.
- When joining more than two strips together, press the seams after attaching each strip. You are more likely to get bowing if you leave it until your strip unit is complete before pressing.
- Each seam must be pressed flat before another seam is sewn across it. Unless there is a special reason for not doing so, seams are pressed towards the darker fabric. The main criteria when joining seams, however, is to have the seam allowances going in the opposite direction to each other as they then nest together without bulk. Your patchwork will lie flat and your seam intersections will be accurate.

PINNING

Don't underestimate the benefits of pinning. When you have to align a seam it is important to insert pins to stop any movement when sewing. Long, fine pins with flat heads are recommended as they will go through the layers of fabric easily and allow you to sew up to and over them.

Seams should always be pressed in opposite directions so they will nest together nicely. Insert a pin either at right angles or diagonally through the seam intersection ensuring that the seams are matching perfectly. When sewing, do not remove the pin too early as your fabric might shift and your seams will not be perfectly aligned.

CHAIN PIECING

Chain piecing is the technique of feeding a series of pieces through the sewing machine without lifting the presser foot and without cutting the thread between each piece. Always chain piece when you can – it saves time and thread. Once your chain is complete simply snip the thread between the fabric pieces.

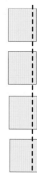

When chain piecing shapes other than squares and rectangles it is sometimes preferable when finishing one shape, to lift the presser foot slightly and reposition on the next shape, still leaving the thread uncut.

REMOVING DOG EARS

A dog ear is the excess piece of fabric that overlaps past the seam allowance when sewing triangles to other shapes. Dog ears should always be cut off to reduce bulk. They can be trimmed using a rotary cutter although snipping with small sharp scissors is quicker. Make sure you are trimming the points parallel to the straight edge of the triangle.

JOINING BORDER AND BINDING STRIPS

If you need to join strips for your borders and binding, you may choose to join them with a diagonal seam to make them less noticeable. Press the seams open.

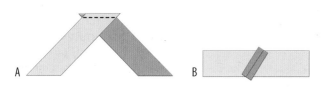

ADDING BORDERS

The fabric requirements in this book all assume you are going to be sewing straight rather than mitred borders. If you intend to have mitred borders please add sufficient extra fabric for this.

ADDING STRAIGHT BORDERS

1 Determine the vertical measurement from top to bottom through the centre of your quilt top. Cut two side border strips to this measurement. Mark the halves and quarters of one quilt side and one border with pins. Placing right sides together and matching the pins, stitch the quilt and border together, easing the quilt side to fit where necessary. Repeat on the opposite side. Press seams open.

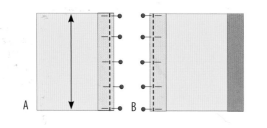

2 Determine the horizontal measurement from side to side across the centre of the quilt top. Cut two top and bottom border strips to this measurement and add to the quilt top in the same manner.

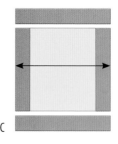

ADDING MITRED BORDERS

If you wish to create mitred borders rather than straight borders follow these instructions.

1 Measure the length and width of the quilt and cut two border strips the length of the quilt plus twice the width of the border, and then cut two border strips the width of the quilt plus twice the width of the border.

2 Sew the border strips to the quilt beginning and ending ¼in away from the corners, back stitching to secure at either end. Begin your sewing right next to where you have finished sewing your previous border but ensure your stitching doesn't overlap. When you have sewn your four borders, press and lay the quilt out on a flat surface, with the reverse side of the quilt up.

3 Fold the top border up and align it with the side border. Press the resulting 45-degree line that starts at the ¼in stop and runs to the outside edge of the border.

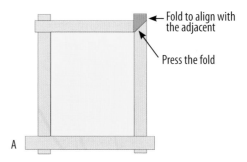

Fold to align with the adjacent

Press the fold

4 Now lift the side border above the top border and fold it to align with the top border. Press it to create a 45-degree line. Repeat with all four corners.

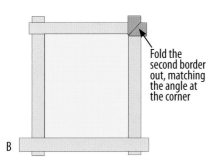

Fold the second border out, matching the angle at the corner

B

5 Align the horizontal and vertical borders in one corner by folding the quilt diagonally and stitching along the pressed 45-degree line to form the mitre, back stitching at either end. Trim the excess border fabric ¼in from your sewn line. Repeat with the other three corners.

QUILTING

Quilting stitches hold the patchwork top, wadding (batting) and backing together and create texture over your finished patchwork. The choice is yours whether you hand quilt, machine quilt or send the quilt off to a longarm quilting service. There are many books dedicated to the techniques of hand and machine quilting but the basic procedure is as follows.

1 With the aid of templates or a ruler, mark out the quilting lines on the patchwork top.

2 Cut the backing fabric and wadding at least 4in larger all around than the patchwork top. Pin or tack the layers together to prepare them for quilting.

3 Quilt either by hand or by machine. Remove any quilting marks on completion of the quilting.

BINDING A QUILT

The fabric requirements in this book are for a 2½in double-fold French binding cut on the straight grain.

1 Trim the excess backing and wadding so that the edges are even with the top of the quilt.

2 Join your binding strips into a continuous length, making sure there is sufficient to go around the quilt plus 8in–10in for corners and overlapping ends. With wrong sides together, press the binding in half lengthways. Fold and press under ½in to neaten the edge at the end where you will start sewing.

3 On the right side of the quilt and starting about 12in away from a corner, align the edges of the double thickness binding with the edge of the quilt so that the cut edges are towards the edges of the quilt and pin to hold in place. Sew with a ¼in seam allowance, leaving the first inch open. At the first corner, stop ¼in from the edge of the fabric and back stitch (A). Lift needle and presser foot and fold the binding upwards (B). Fold the binding again but downwards (C). Stitch from the edge to ¼in from the next corner and repeat the turn.

4 Continue all around the quilt working each corner in the same way. When you come to the starting point, cut the binding, fold under the cut edge and overlap at the starting point.

5 Fold the binding over to the back of the quilt and hand stitch it in place all round, folding the binding at each corner to form a neat mitre.

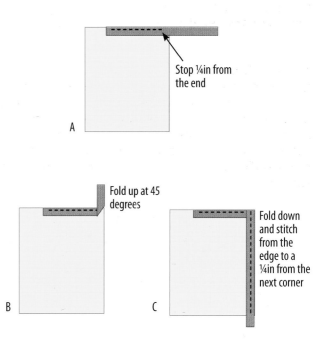

Stop ¼in from the end

A

Fold up at 45 degrees

B

Fold down and stitch from the edge to a ¼in from the next corner

C

MAKING A LARGER QUILT

If you want to make a larger version of any of the quilts in the book, refer to the Vital Statistics of the quilt, which shows the block size, the number of blocks, how the blocks are set plus the size of border used. You can then calculate your requirements for a larger quilt.

SETTING ON POINT

Any block can take on a totally new look when set on point and you might like to try one of the quilts to see what it looks like on point. For this reason we have included information for setting quilts on point. Some people are a little daunted as there are a few things to take into consideration but here is all you need to know.

HOW WIDE WILL MY BLOCKS BE WHEN SET ON POINT?

To calculate the measurement of the block from point to point you multiply the size of the finished block by 1.414. Example: a 12in block will measure 12in x 1.414 which is 16.97in – just under 17in. Now you can calculate how many blocks you need for your quilt.

HOW DO I PIECE BLOCKS ON POINT?

Piece rows diagonally, starting at a corner. Triangles have to be added to the end of each row before joining the rows and these are called setting triangles.

HOW DO I CALCULATE WHAT SIZE SETTING TRIANGLES TO CUT?

Setting triangles form the outside of your quilt and need to have the straight of grain on the outside edge to prevent stretching. To ensure this, these triangles are formed from quarter-square triangles, i.e., a square cut into four. The measurement for this is: Diagonal Block Size + 1¼in. Example: a 12in block (diagonal measurement approximately 17in) should be 18¼in.

Corners triangles are added last. They also need to have the outside edge on the straight of grain so these should be cut from half-square triangles. To calculate the size of square to cut in half, divide the finished size of your block by 1.414 then add ⅞in. Example: a 12in block would be 12in divided by 1.414 = 8.49in + ⅞in (0.88) = 9.37in (or 9½in as it can be trimmed later).

Most diagonal quilts start off with one block and in each row thereafter the number of blocks increases by two. All rows contain an odd number of blocks. To calculate the finished size of the quilt, you count the number of diagonals across and multiply this by the diagonal measurement of the block. Do the same with the number of blocks down and multiply this by the diagonal measurement of the block.

If you want a rectangular quilt instead of a square one, you count the number of blocks in the row that establishes the width and repeat that number in following rows until the desired length is established.

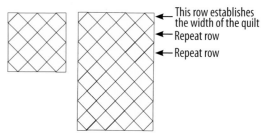

This row establishes the width of the quilt
← Repeat row
← Repeat row

CALCULATING BACKING FABRIC

The patterns do not include backing requirements as many people like to use extra wide backing fabric to avoid joins.

USING 60IN WIDE FABRIC

This is a simple calculation as to how much you need to buy. Example: your quilt is 54in x 72in. Your backing needs to be 3in larger all round so your backing measurement is 60in x 78in. If you have found 60in wide backing, then you would buy the length which is 78in. However, if you have found 90in wide backing, you can turn it round and you would only have to buy the width of 60in.

USING 42IN WIDE FABRIC

You will need to have a join or joins in order to get the required measurement unless the backing measurement for your quilt is 42in or less on one side. If your backing measurement is less than 42in then you need only buy one length.

Using the previous example, if your backing measurement is 60in x 78in, you will have to have one seam somewhere in your backing. If you join two lengths of 42in fabric together your new fabric measurement will be 84in (less a little for the seam). This would be sufficient for the length of your quilt so you would need to buy twice the width, i.e. 60in x 2 = 120in. Your seam will run horizontal.

If your quilt length is more than your new backing fabric measurement of 84in you will need to use the measurement of 84in for the width of your quilt and you will have to buy twice the length. Your seam will then run vertical.

LABELLING YOUR QUILT

When you have finished your quilt it is important to label it even if the information you put on the label is just your name and the date. When looking at antique quilts it is always interesting to piece together information about the quilt, so you can be sure that any extra information you put on the label will be of immense interest to quilters of the future. For example, you could say why you made the quilt and who it was for, or for what special occasion.

Labels can be as ornate as you like, but a very simple and quick method is to write on a piece of calico with a permanent marker pen and then appliqué this to the back of your quilt.

Useful Contacts

Creative Grids (UK) Ltd
Unit 1J, Peckleton Lane Business Park,
Peckleton Lane, Peckleton,
Leicester LE9 7RN, UK
Tel: 01455 828667
www.creativegrids.com

Janome UK Ltd
Janome Centre, Southside,
Stockport, Cheshire SK6 2SP, UK
Tel: 0161 666 6011
www.janome.com

Moda Fabrics/United Notions
13800 Hutton Drive, Dallas,
Texas 75234, USA
Tel: 800-527-9447
www.modafabrics.com

The Quilt Room
Shop & Mail Order
37–39 High Street, Dorking,
Surrey RH4 1AR, UK
Tel: 01306 877307
www.quiltroom.co.uk

Winbourne Fabrics Ltd
(Moda's UK Distributor)
Unit 3A, Forge Way, Knypersley,
Stoke on Trent ST8 7DN, UK
www.winbournefabrics.co.uk

RUCraft
RUCraft is an online craft shop,
with a beautiful array of sewing fabrics.
www.rucraft.co.uk

Acknowledgments

Pam and Nicky would firstly like to thank Mark Dunn at Moda for his continued support and for allowing them to use the name jelly roll in the title and throughout the book. Thanks also go to Lissa Alexander, Susan Rogers and the whole team at Moda.

Their thanks also go to the loyal team of staff at The Quilt Room who keep The Quilt Room running smoothly when Pam and Nicky are rushing to meet tight deadlines. Special thanks to Rosemary Miller, Pam's business partner for many years, for lending some of her antique quilts for this project. Together Pam and Rosemary bought many antique quilts and on Rosemary's retirement when the collection was split they alternated in choosing their favourites to keep – it was a difficult choice!

Thanks to Matt and Rachel Cross of Creative Grids for allowing them to feature the stunning Tumbling Blocks quilt. Knowing how much both Pam and Nicky loved it, they still can't believe Matt and Rachel trusted them enough to return it to them! Thanks also to Jenny Hutchison and Barbara Chainey for their expertise in dating the antique quilts.

Last but not least, special thanks to Pam's husband Nick and to Nicky's husband Rob for looking after sheep, chickens, guinea fowl, dogs and a little boy, plus attending to everything else that needs to be done when deadlines are being met and computers and sewing machines are working overtime!

About the Authors

Pam Lintott opened her shop, The Quilt Room, in 1981, which she still runs today, along with her daughter Nicky. Pam is the author of *The Quilt Room Patchwork & Quilting Workshops*, as well as *The Quilter's Workbook*. The Quilt Room celebrated its 30th anniversary last year and is now starting on its journey towards the next 30 years! It is housed in a 15th century inn located in the historic market town of Dorking, Surrey just south of London, UK.

Antique to Heirloom Jelly Roll Quilts is Pam and Nicky's eighth book for David & Charles following on from *Jelly Roll Dreams, More Layer Cake, Jelly Roll & Charm Quilts, Jelly Roll Sampler Quilts, Two from One Jelly Roll Quilts, Jelly Roll Inspirations, Layer Cake, Jelly Roll & Charm Quilts,* and their phenomenally successful *Jelly Roll Quilts*. See www.rucraft.co.uk for information on how to obtain these books.

INDEX

A DAVID & CHARLES BOOK
© F&W Media International, Ltd 2012

David & Charles is an imprint of F&W Media International, Ltd
Brunel House, Forde Close, Newton Abbot, TQ12 4PU, UK

F&W Media International, Ltd is a subsidiary of F+W Media, Inc
10151 Carver Road, Cincinnati OH45242, USA

Text and Designs © Pam and Nicky Lintott 2012
Layout and Photography © F&W Media International, Ltd 2012

First published in the UK and USA in 2012

Names of manufacturers and product ranges are provided for
the information of readers, with no intention to infringe copyright
or trademarks.

A catalogue record for this book is available from the British Library.

ISBN-13: 978-1-4463-0182-1 paperback
ISBN-10: 1-4463-0182-6 paperback

Paperback edition printed in China by RR Donnelley for:
F&W Media International, Ltd
Brunel House, Forde Close, Newton Abbot, TQ12 4PU, UK

10 9 8 7 6 5 4 3 2 1

Acquisitions Editor: Katy Denny
Editor: James Brooks
Project Editor: Lin Clements
Art Editor: Jodie Lystor
Photographer: Lorna Yabsley
Production Manager: Bev Richardson

F+W Media publishes high quality books on a wide range of subjects.
For more great book ideas visit: **www.rucraft.co.uk**